Building & Maintaining An

ALWAYS
POSITIVE
ATTITUDE

In Your Business…

A Compilation

JACK DAUGHERY

JIM DORNAN

JIM FLOOR

HAL GOOCH

BRIAN AND MARG HAYES

BURKE HEDGES

DR. RON JENSON

BEVERLY SALLEE

TIM TEMPLETON

DOUG WEAD

D0110175

Building & Maintaining
An Always Positive Attitude
In Your Business

© Future Achievement International/
MasterTrack International

All Rights Reserved

Published By:

Future Achievement International®

MasterTrack International

ISBN 0-9709483-5-2

Table of Contents

Introduction

W e have all seen the advertisements-lose 10 pounds in 30 days. Or is it 30 pounds in 10 days? Of course, losing weight-10 pounds or 30 pounds-isn't that simple. Anybody on a diet knows that. You need a plan, and you need persistence.

But most of all, you need to change your behavior.

So, we're going to put you on a diet. No more servings of fear, anxiety, dread and helplessness. Stop and think about how that weighs you down. Let's get rid of all those negatives you've been carrying around. Imagine how much lighter you'll be, how much better you'll feel.

Sleek. Energized. Confident.

Always positive...

This book will give you a brand new attitude...an *always positive* attitude. You'll have some of the biggest names in business, right there beside you, telling you exactly how to do it:

- Jim Dornan, *A Healthy Self Image*
- Hal Gooch, *Identify your What & Why*
- Beverly Sallee, *Visualize the Finish Line*
- Jack Daughery, *Self-Discipline Creates an Always Positive Attitude*
- Jim Floor, *Get Out of the Vacuum – and Build*
- Brian and Marg Hays, *Make It Happen*

These authors and speakers will inspire and encourage you with specific take-away examples and steps to develop and maintain an *always positive* attitude:

- Dr. Ron Jenson, *The Life Changing Impact of Mentors-Powerful Influences in Positive Thinking* and *Living a Principle-centered Life*
- Doug Wead, *Hitting the Wall*
- Burke Hedges, *The Power of a To Do List*
- Tim Templeton, *A Brand New Attitude - Never Know Fail*

Together, we will give you a way to make your own plan for an *always positive* attitude. We will help you develop the persistence you'll need to stick with it. Together, we'll change your unwanted behavior patterns, charting a direction for success.

This book outlines our personal hurdles and insights, detailing how we maintained the proper attitude in all circumstances, and ultimately found success in the business. Each of us has authored a chapter outlining a specific principle that will assist you in developing and maintaining an *always positive* attitude in your business. We'll give you specific advice and encouragement to help you achieve and maintain an *always positive* attitude as you build your business.

More to the point, these chapters are offered as a guidebook and reference manual. Read through the book, and then refer back to its wisdom as you build up your personal, rock-solid foundational attitude to attain your personal goals. This handbook of general encouragement and specific steps will assist you.

We've all been there ourselves. We've experienced what you're going through right now. We'll tell you what worked for us-the specific steps it took to develop and maintain an *always positive* attitude. We make this promise-take the time to read our stories for new or additional insights, and you'll be able to apply them immediately when you finish this book.

So, let's get started.

-Tim Templeton

1

A Brand New Attitude

By Tim Templeton

"The greatest revolution of our generation is the discovery that human beings, by changing the inner attitudes of their minds, can change the outer aspects of their lives."
- William James

Changing our behavior is the key to controlling our attitudes. Throughout my years of observing the best and brightest in the industry, I have noted that the majority of leaders who have achieved success in business project a consistent behavioral pattern - an *always positive* attitude.

The people who are *always positive* have learned how to avoid all the negatives in their lives. It's a series of choices and it's something that they do every day. So, as long as we're all making choices, let's make the right ones. Let's learn from the *always positive* people in business – let's mold our personal characteristics, attitudes, and mindsets while maintaining our individuality, gifts, and skill-sets. We'll be different people, looking at ourselves in a different way.

With this brand new attitude, we'll move through our world with more confidence and control. We can project that take-charge attitude at work, but remain patient and complacent at home with our families. When you recognize and understand its power, it will work for you. It's been verified by independent research. Inscape Publishing, publishers of the D.I.S.C. personality profile, has conducted a number of studies that show you have the ability to change your behavioral pattern.

Let me say that again-it is a proven scientific fact that we all have the ability to change our behavioral patterns. By possessing the ability to change your behavior, you will guarantee your success. You will reach your personal goals-whoever you are.

It doesn't take a big salary or a fancy corporate title. It doesn't matter if you've been in business for a while, or if you're just getting started. Each and every one of us has the ability to change in order to develop an attitude that will be the foundation of our success in business. Our new attitudes will bring in new business.

Reducing stress

Stress is something we all get the "joy" of experiencing throughout our lives. It helps build character in certain situations, but it can be debilitating when we experience it over a prolonged period of time. One of the best exercises I have ever experienced in understanding how to get a handle on controlling stress was through a close friend and fellow trainer, Craig Case.

Craig led a custom planner division for FranklinCovey that introduced the many new innovations in the industry. He taught individuals in more than 20 countries techniques on how to reduce stress by gaining control over certain events that go on in your day. Craig has "been there and done that."

I licensed the Franklin Planner that incorporated a system to produce more referrals for independent business owners. Through this experience I first met Craig; it was an unforgettable encounter. Craig is six foot six inches tall and 280 pounds. I'm five-foot-seven and 190 pounds. I *really* looked up to Craig, like almost everybody else. On occasion to the delight of the crowd, I have stood on a chair so I could look *down* on Craig - almost. He is an imposing figure in front of any audience. Over the years and through a number of shared experiences, we became close friends and trained together in front of a number of groups.

90-Day Plan of Action

A company contracted with me to develop a 1½ day training program, to get their new and existing independent distributors focused and productive with a simple but effective 90-Day Plan of Action. I asked Craig to join me and create a variation to the program he taught – helping business owners get a handle on stress, reduce it, and develop the clear thinking needed to map out a plan of action. Here's how it worked with one couple that attended the program.

James and Lynn

James and Lynn came to the training program with a dogged determination to succeed. They also were experiencing the usual questions that added to their stress:

- Would it work for them?
- Why did it seem so easy for others?
- Should they take the time and money to attend?

They had pushed off the usual negative demons and decided to make a "push" in their business. They made the investment and traveled across several states to attend with an open mind.

In control or out of control?

I started the program by announcing that the left side of the room would represent "Out of Control" and the right side represented "Control." Using the flip chart-size sticky notes, I wrote out both phrases and quickly stuck one on each side of the room.

"Throughout our life," I told the group, "sometimes we're in control and other times we feel we are out of control." I walked over to the No Control poster, because I had a perfect example to share.

"Last winter, I was in Big Bear Lake on a ski and snowboard weekend with my family," I began. "We were fortunate enough to experience a storm with six inches of new snow, just right for our next day on the slopes.

"There was just one problem. I didn't put chains on my tires. I was slipping and sliding down the main thoroughfare in my van, barely able to see the road because of the weather. Suddenly, I saw the red brake lights from a line of cars just 20 feet in front of me! I jammed on my brakes and turned the wheel, feeling that familiar churn in my stomach. A thousand thoughts ran through my mind as I slid to a stop less than an inch from the last car in line.

"I was definitely out of control," I concluded. Then, I asked the audience, "how many of you have ever been in a situation where you have been out of control?" Almost everyone raised a hand. James and Lynn had their hands in the air, too.

Looking at James and Lynn, I asked another question. "What type of emotions did you experience when you felt out of control?"

"Fear, anxiety," they offered.

Others yelled, "dread, helplessness."

I quickly wrote down the words they associated with the phrase "No Control."

Then I walked to the other side of the room, next to the sheet titled, "Control." I smiled and said, "you just enrolled five new individuals this week, received the largest commission check to date, and suddenly you can actually see yourself quitting the full-time work that you dread Monday morning. For the first time ever, you have 'more money than month'... how does that make you feel?"

The responses came with more energy and smiles. One lady yelled out, "I fe-eel good." James Brown couldn't have said it better.

"Less stress," another said.

"I'm in control," a young man offered.

"I have more energy," James said.

"Now, I have a positive attitude," said Lynn.

I wrote the words, *more energy, less stress, feel good, in control, positive attitude*, on the sheet labeled Control.

Gaining control

I stood with my hands raised and positioned exactly between the two signs. "Now, where do we spend most of our lives, in control or out of control?" I asked. The crowd, with James and Lynn pointing the way, directed me to the "No Control" sign.

I smiled and said, "here is what my friend Craig taught me after teaching time management over 10 years. You can't manage time, it's a misnomer, and it waits for no one. It just continues going and going with no way to control it. What you can control are certain events.

"In doing so, you will experience the everyday feeling of being in control, as opposed to those we talked about when you are out of control. Time management is best described as event control," I continued. "What we are going to do today is identify those events that you can control."

The tool and the answer

"Here's the exciting part for me, the part where I show you how to change your attitude," I told the crowd. "I will show you how to construct a simple and effective 90-Day Plan of Action."

I moved over to the Control side of the room. "With this new plan, you will know where you are going every day of every month. Those you lead will now have a reason to follow you. Furthermore, you will have the ability to teach others in your organization to do the same, thereby duplicating yourself and start enjoying what capitalism promises."

The sudden expression on James and Lynn's face was a *light bulb moment* for both of them. "This is so simple, to simple, can it be that simple?" they asked, with hope in their eyes.

"Absolutely," I stated, "but first you have to understand your 'why,' the things that are your motivating factors."

Understanding your "why"

We all want control, because it gives us the ability to achieve our goals. But first, we need to experience the emotions associated with being in control. We must first understand our *why*. I knew Lynn would be perfect for my next demonstration.

"I need a volunteer," I said. I smiled and walked right over to her. Lynn hesitated, but the crowd urged her on. Everyone clapped when she finally got up. As she turned to the audience, I asked her, "Lynn, you have a child under five, don't you?" She was still somewhat intimidated by the large group, but she nodded her head. "Tell us about your child," I continued. It's an offer no parent can refuse.

"His name is Josh, and he's four this month," she said with love in her voice. "He's our only son and is a real sweetheart. James and I tried for a long time to have a child and we feel...no, we are certain he was an absolute gift from God."

James beamed as Lynn described their son. "That's great, Lynn," I said. "Now, let me ask you a question. Have you ever been to the Golden Gate Bridge in San Francisco?"

She nodded her head again. "For those of you who've never seen it," I said, "let me give you some facts about the bridge. It spans a bay that's more than a mile in length. It's 746 feet tall, from the water level to the top of both bridge towers. Those towers are about 60 feet wide. If you were to stand on top of one of those towers and look down at the water, people look like ants on the boats that pass underneath.

"The bridge is extremely heavy, due to the 61,500-ton load from the cables; it's designed to sway back and forth to compensate for the high winds and weight. In a stiff wind, it will actually swing about five feet side to side."

The bridge is an engineering marvel, but I was going to make it personal. "Lynn, let me ask you another question," I said, as I walked away from her. "Do you know what an I beam is?"

"It's used in construction, isn't it?" she replied.

"Yes, that's right," I said, motioning with my hands. "It's shaped in the form of a capital I. It's 12 inches high and six inches wide."

I quickly faced the audience and called out, "anybody carrying a $100 bill in their wallet?" A few raised their hands and I asked John, a successful leader, if I could borrow his.

"You'll get it back... maybe."

Everyone chuckled as I snatched it from him. I walked back to where I had been standing and turned toward Lynn.

"Imagine for a moment that this I-beam, 60 feet in length, was laid on the floor between us," I said. "Would you walk across it for the $100 bill I'm holding up?"

"You bet," she beamed, as everyone looked back at John and laughed.

"It will be coming out of your fee," John shot back as the laughter was redirected my way.

"I understand," I replied. "But wait, Lynn. Before you walk across the I-beam, I'm going to put it across the top of one of the towers that span the Golden Gate Bridge...746 feet above the water.

"Oh, and the entire bridge is swaying about five feet in both directions, because of the wind." I started to sway back and forth with my hands in the air. I looked at Lynn and continued, "come on, sway with me. We're on top of the Golden Gate Bridge!"

Everybody laughed.

"Will you cross the I beam now for $100 dollars?" I asked Lynn.

"No way," she deadpanned.

"How about for $100,000? Would you cross it for that much?"

"No, I don't want to die," she said.

"How about a million dollars?"

"No."

"What if I throw in a Winnebago?" The audience howled.

What will motivate you cross the I-beam?

I faced the audience, still positioned across from Lynn. We were still on top of our imaginary bridge. "Let's see if we can get Lynn to cross the I-beam," I said. "Lynn, imagine for a moment that we're on top of the Golden Gate, but now I have little Josh standing next to me."

Everyone in the audience got very quiet and Lynn's face took on a very serious demeanor. "I'm holding Josh by the collar and I'm going to let him go over the side, unless you cross the I-beam.

"Will you cross the I-beam now?"

"You better believe I will and you're going over as soon as I get there!" she said.

"I believe you, Lynn," I said, smiling. "Let's give her a big round of applause."

What matters most to you?

As Lynn returned to her seat, I brought it all home to the audience. "If we get in touch with our motivating factors, our 'why' - the things that matter most to us in life - and then tie them to events we can control, we have an opportunity to achieve our goals.

"What I would like you to do now is to take a few moments and jot down what matters most to you. What are the motivating factors in your life?

What is your 'why?' Write down whatever it might be, such as a specific amount of money to pay your debts, more time with a spouse or child.

"Perhaps it's having enough time on your hands and enough freedom to simply get in shape and exercise daily. Be specific." I watched closely as the group started writing immediately. While classical music filled the air, James and Lynn were writing and stopping to compare notes - they were really pulling together as a team.

"Times up, who wants to share?" I asked. A number of individuals encouraged by the group camaraderie shared their specific *whys*. Some shed tears because of their new-found answers, while others experienced a new-found confidence because of the plan that was developing before them.

Every time I conduct one of these training sessions, I hear the same answers: financial independence to leave a current job, more time with family and friends, focus on health and quality of life. The difference was that they had become identified and personalized for the members of this audience.

Building a plan around your why

During the break, there was a lot of discussion in the hallway regarding focus, goals and attitude. When we started up again, I recapped the steps and thoughts we had experienced together, to keep everyone on track.

"In review of this morning's session, I want everyone to remember where we have been and know where we are going. When you leave here today, you'll have completed a 90-day plan that will change your business forever.

"This plan will outline key things that you decide you want to do, events you can control and accomplish. In doing so, you will move throughout your day with rigorous focus. That will reduce stress, and give you more energy to be more productive. That translates into money.

"Our next step is to outline an achievable goal, identify the events necessary to complete the goal and drive the plan with the right attitude – every day. We refer to it as building your business with an *always positive* attitude. In order to fulfill that goal, we have spent considerable time understanding our motivating factors, the things that push us internally to get to where want to get."

I moved over to the Control side of the room. "By identifying these things, are you gaining control?" I asked. I received an emphatic "yes!" James and Lynn were leading the charge.

Visualize the goal line

"Our next step is to write an achievable 90-day goal. The operative word here is *achievable*. Dr. Norman Vincent Peale wrote a lot about positive thought and goals. His instruction was to set a goal that was no more than 10% above your comfort zone. For our purposes here today, this goal should be a specific dollar amount you would like to earn within 90 days.

"It's important to understand that your goal should be within striking distance if you apply yourself. I want the paper on which it is written to become the icon for your success, not the icon for your failure. We will take several minutes to write out the goal on the forms provided. Start now."

James motioned to me that he had a question. I walked across the room, with Mozart still playing in the background. Everyone was busy with scribing his or her goals.

"I want to make sure we write something we can really achieve," he said. Lynn nodded in agreement, adding, "we've set goals before, but they never quite worked out. I think they were too grandiose and we didn't tie a plan to them."

I understood completely. "This time, I want you to be able to see the finish line. Also, make sure you see several stepping stones that you can control to get there." These two were already thinking about the next level, and I loved it.

"Times up, who wants to run the risk and share their goal with the rest of the group?" Everyone sat quietly waiting for someone else to make the move.

Finally, Lynn stood up and said, "we'll share ours. James and I developed a goal we both feel we can achieve. Tim told us to speak like it's already happened, so here goes. Three months have passed and we have reached our goal of $4000 per month in commissions. We have just opened Josh's college fund with $500.

"The exhilaration we feel for achieving our goal is something we have never experienced before. We love that feeling, and want to continue growing. We have more energy and feel a sense of confidence and control in regards to our future. We are definitely fired up!"

Everyone in the audience applauded, feeling the newfound confidence Lynn described. It seemed like she actually could see the finish line. It was so real; I could feel a chill running down my back. Several more in the audience shared their goals with the same response from the audience.

A goal is a dream with a deadline

"Now, our next step is planning one key event each month. You want to be able to hitch your wagon to this event. Every working day, with your key event in place, you'll have the ability to focus on it. See the event as the vehicle that will help you achieve your 90-day goal. Every action, call or contact you make will point to achieving success in your defined event.

Now, identify your event, is it a specific number of presentations, group presentation, calls for appointments? Write it down now."

I walked to the Control side of the room again. "Is the event something you can control?" I asked.

"Yes!" was the loud response.

Short term goals

"Gang, we're almost there," I pleaded. "Stay with me. Our last step this morning is to list several weekly short-term goals and next steps, as they relate to our monthly event.

Again, these are simple achievable goals that you decide on for yourself. "This is your plan based on your motivating factors. The action steps you list and complete each week next to the box provided on your 90-Day Plan will receive a big checkmark. Keeping up with these short term goals is what's going to give you the ability to feel in control and remain always positive in regards to building your business."

A personalized Plan of Action

As the morning concluded, everyone in the room had a finished personalized plan that they could take home and attach to their office wall. They could look at it every day. Once a month, they could update the plan and add 30 more days to it.

James and Lynn were particularly excited about the day's events, because they had several people who where part of their business in attendance. They now possessed their own plan. They saw the plan as the common denominator they could use in their weekly meetings with their team for regular planning purposes, to keep everyone motivated and on track.

90 days later

I received the call from James – almost three months to the day after he and Lynn completing their first 90-day plan. "Tim," he exclaimed, "we did it, we achieved our financial goal!"

"Great, James," I said. "What was the single biggest factor?"

"The plan," he shouted over the phone. "We finally had a plan, so we could keep everyone on track. I have duplicated your training three times with my organization and everyone has a 90-Day Plan. We coach everyone, based on his or her own personal plan!

"The fact that each person created achievable goals all tied to their own personal *why* has made the difference. We definitely are in an *always positive* state of mind in regards to building our business!"

Simple application

The application for you and your business is fairly straightforward. Here's a simple outline you can start on after reading the rest of these chapters. Each leader and author will give you an insight or suggestion that will resonate with you. Incorporate those that resonate and apply it to your business. The biggest compliment you can give any author is the application of his or her advice. When applying a 90-Day Plan of Action strategy, remember:

1. Identify the events that you can control and manage them (number of contacts in a day, presentations, etc.)

2. Get in touch with your personal *why* in specific terms. What will make you cross the I-beam?

3. Develop a simple 90-Day Plan of Action. Start with an achievable goal tied to a to dollar amount

4. Develop and commit to a monthly key event (talk with others you are associated with to help define Key Event)

5. Detail weekly short-term goals that lead up to your monthly Key Event

6. Share your goals with others on your team for accountability and camaraderie

7. Stay the Course

The Leaders and Authors who share in the next chapters are all champions. They know how to develop and maintain an *always positive* attitude in building your business. Enjoy their advice and share it with others.

Remember, you are in control of your brand new attitude – your *always positive* attitude!

2

A Healthy Self Image

By Jim Dornan

"One way to find out is to look in a mirror. Look there, and we'll see someone's dearly beloved, someone warm and honest and trusting and human and loving and thoughtful; foolish sometimes, and sometimes wise. There we'll see one who can encourage and coax and inspire another human being to live to her very best, to reach the highest he can dare imagine."

-Richard Bach

It may come as a surprise to discover this, but one of the most difficult things to achieve and maintain in life is a healthy and positive self- image. As we pursue our individual dreams and goals, we must discover the principles that lead to a solid foundation.

Our self-image, the true picture and value we place on ourselves, is one of those very important foundations. Any success built on false perceptions or one relying on artificial symbols of worth and confidence will ultimately lead to frustration or failure.

Misconceptions

In this chapter, I will attempt to shed some light on these principles and offer some cautions about common misconceptions. It is certainly true that our current culture is filled with messages that try to convince us that if we will simply try a certain product, our life will be complete. Advertisers constantly remind us that we can be more "socially acceptable" if we just drive their brand of car or wear their clothes, or drink their beverages. The problem is that a healthy self- image is far more complex than being "cool."

Our world is full of people who seem to have it all together – on the outside. But on the inside, they are filled with doubt and insecurities. Many people are trapped in this futile game of trying to appear confident by wearing the "right" clothes and hanging with the "right" group. But on the inside, they're acting – playing a part.

Here's the truth: a healthy self-image is deeper, more enduring and less fragile than simply the latest fad. To be happy and truly successful, we need a positive, healthy self-image. It's not about pleasing others, or following popular trends. It's about knowing:

✓ Who you are
✓ Where you are going
✓ What you stand for

In this process, you'll discover areas where you already excel, or have the potential to achieve greatness (we all have plenty of each.) You'll also learn to recognize areas where you could use a little improvement, and start that process (we all have those, too).

A healthy self-image is about being the best you can be. It is not about comparing yourself to others, or pursuing perfection. We all experience success and failure in our lives. It's all about how you handle those triumphs and setbacks.

As you develop your healthy self-image, you'll discover the balance between:

- A sense of peace
- A sense of purpose
- A sense of humor

What are we focused on?

As I have observed people, it seems there are three psychological characteristics of human behavior:

1. **Superiority**: I must see myself and project myself in such a way as to confirm that I have no weaknesses or flaws. I am the strongest, the smartest, and the "coolest," the most successful person in the group. This is "positive," but not healthy.

2. **Inferiority**: I see myself as less talented, less attractive, less successful than anyone else. I see their strengths against my weaknesses. I always want to obtain the qualities I lack or see in others, and assume my gifts are insignificant. This is neither positive nor healthy.

3. **Balanced**: I recognize that I have God-given strengths or gifts that can be used to pursue my goals, and I acknowledge the gifts of others without fear of reducing my value. I work on improving, but have no illusions about perfection. This is healthy and positive, and it will lead to a life of significance and satisfaction.

The problem is that we all have pride. We all have egos, and we want to be seen by others as strong, attractive and successful. However, we seem to have a built-in tendency to focus on our weaknesses and minimize our gifts.

Perhaps we feel this is humility. But I see it as simply unhealthy. Most of us are aware of our weaknesses and failures - painfully aware. In fact, we rehearse them over and over in our minds. It soon becomes easier to be aware of weakness and failure, with all that practice.

At the same time, we recognize the strengths we see in others. We admire them, so it's not too difficult to put those people on a pedestal. We tend to balance our failings with their successes. Naturally, we don't come out very well. In those kinds of comparisons, we hardly ever measure up.

But our negative thoughts and feelings didn't just pop into our hearts and minds one day. Where do negative thoughts and feelings come from? Were we born with them? Is it a question of temperament? Environment? My horoscope? The position of the moon?

Feelings of inadequacy may have first struck us when we were very young, with a childhood embarrassment that may still haunt us when we think about it. Most of us could make a list without thinking twice. Taunts from schoolmates, parents or teachers may have stayed with us all through our lives.

"Look at little Four-Eyes!"

"Oh, you're still here, Chubby,"

"Hey, Shorty, stand up!"

"You Dummy!"

We remember every rejection, every embarrassment, and every nickname as though they were dragging along behind us on a string. But the people who say and do those things to us? The tragedy is that those people who say or do those things to us typically never even remember them.

Most of us take ourselves far too seriously, and spend too much time thinking about "what others think." Actually, others think about you far less than you can imagine. Have you ever noticed when people look at a picture of themselves? They say, "That looks horrible."

But it looks just like them.

Occasionally, it is true that a picture is unflattering. But often, it's just someone who is overly obsessed with his or her own 'image'.

"My hair isn't right."

"I look fat."

You get the idea.

Let's say this person is pictured in a group. Does this person think that way about all the other people in the picture?

No. This person isn't paying any attention to *them*.

And no one's paying that much attention to you, either!

Here's the point. A good self-image goes beyond appearances. We need to learn to accept ourselves (bald head and all). Then, we work on the inner things that create a healthy self-image. We will attract others – not by what's on the outside, but what's on the inside.

That's the formula for success.

Here's a great example:

Our son, Eric, has been a constant source of inspiration to our family. At birth, Eric was diagnosed with Spina Bifida, a defect in the spinal chord or central nervous system. The condition has many complications. He was required to endure 11 brain surgeries in his first year of life. By the time Eric was a teenager, he had 30 brain operations and suffers from seizures as well as bladder and kidney problems.

However, Eric's attitude about his medical problems has always been amazing to those around him. One time, Eric was sitting at the table in his electric powered wheelchair, taking his anti-seizure medication. Since he had just recovered from one of his many surgeries, his shaved head was covered with stitches and staples.

Eric's brother, David, was sitting next to him. David has worn glasses since he was three, but he suffered from none of Eric's problems. David was wearing his glasses.

At the time, Eric also wore braces. But the orthodontist was going to remove them the very next day.

"Tomorrow, after my braces are off," Eric said to David, "I'll be normal - and you will still be wearing glasses!"

Now there is a person with a positive, healthy self-image.

Eric accepts his limitations (which appear considerable to most of us), and move on to do some verbal sparring with his brother. Eric is very bright, and is well aware of his disabilities. He just chooses to focus on his abilities, not his disabilities.

What's really important?

While our self-image may have been shaped initially by our response to what others said or didn't say, or did or didn't do, we are entirely in control now of the way we regard ourselves. You've probably heard the stories about celebrities and super models, featured in glamorous poses on magazine covers. But they don't think they're attractive.

I don't think this is always false modesty, but rather a deep-seated insecurity that haunts even the most unlikely people. We can be strangely self critical, and it doesn't have to be logical at all. This perception (or obsession) usually revolves around our concept of how we define success.

If we are pursuing *perfection*, or if we are *comparing* ourselves constantly to others, we will undoubtedly feel continually insecure and insufficient for the job at hand. To have the best foundation for long-term success and happiness, we need to learn how to re-define who we are, and what is important.

What are the qualities that will justify a self-image that is truly healthy? What qualities could we pursue that would earn us the right to feel good about ourselves? I honestly believe a healthy, positive self-image begins by knowing that I am part of a picture that reaches far beyond any small frame that I might draw around myself. I am the creation of God, and God does not make mistakes.

Even with our special abilities and talents, we will make mistakes. Occasionally, we may fail. But we must remain confident in our abilities, and persevere. With that as a foundation, we can maintain a focus on the character traits that will always be with us—win or lose.

It seems we should be more concerned with our character, and our integrity and our reputation than with surface qualities. Focus on what's inside, and let other people pursue the externals.

Don't let your circumstances, your abilities (or disabilities) or your past failures discourage you. It's destructive, because it highlights weakness and failure in your life.

Isn't it more valued to be a faithful husband or wife? Or, a loving father? Or a loyal, trusted friend? Of course. Those qualities last a lifetime.

Compare those qualities, which require inner strength, to being popular or beautiful. Those are surface qualities, and some people take a lot of pride in them. But they are simply gifts, rather than character traits. It doesn't take a lot of discipline or integrity to be popular or beautiful.

We all see "ordinary" people, the kind that show up for a hard and honest day's work without fail. They obey the law. They love their families. They serve others with a sense of honor and accountability. Shouldn't they feel great about themselves?

Aren't those the things that matter?

Self-image or self-worship?

I have also learned that there is a dark side to positive thinking and the mindset of a positive self-image. We try to convince ourselves that we are self-sufficient, number one, a genius, beautiful and irresistible. In this scenario, we have merely succumbed to arrogance and pride. Positive self-talk is great - as long as we don't begin to worship ourselves.

We should always remember our limitations. We should always be thankful for our gifts. We should always choose to focus on what we *can* do or *have done*, and not on our failures.

3 STEPS TO SUCCESS

Here are three simple steps in developing and maintaining a healthy, positive self-image:

Identify your assets and strengths and focus on them every day.

- I have a purpose in life
- I am a person of integrity.
- I am a loving, faithful husband and father (wife and mother)
- I am a trustworthy leader
- I am loyal, dependable
- I have a genuine sense of humor (I can laugh at myself, laugh with others)
- I am persistent and resilient
- I am sensitive and compassionate
- I am decisive, optimistic, creative
- I am available and teachable

List the weaknesses that need work

- I need to be more tolerant, or forgiving
- I need to compliment more
- I need to control my anger, jealousy
- I need to remember to smile
- I need to be more disciplined
- I need to be more trusting, optimistic, or positive

"Talking to Yourself"

It's important to focus on what we do well, not on our fears or failures or even on our weaknesses. If you need to work on certain areas in your life, learn to express them in a positive way:

- I'm developing more ability to control my anger or jealousy
- I will do that better next time
- Every day I'm becoming more confident, more decisive, more optimistic, etc.
- I'm a great husband, father, wife, mother, etc.
- I offer great encouragement to people
- My word can be trusted

Write down three or four characteristics that you want to have, and read them daily to affirm them in your mind. You might even put them on your mirror or dashboard, or on the monitor of your computer.

Re-Program Your Computer

The human mind works much like a computer, and it will respond predictably to whatever is put into it. To computer people, GIGO has always meant, "Garbage in, Garbage out." So let's put more good things in, more of what we want.

Imagine that each of us have a glass of water that represented our lives. To symbolize the negatives we've all experienced, red coloring gets added to the water. How dark is the water in your glass?

Some glasses are darker than others are, but all glasses have some discoloration. And once the coloring - negative experiences and images - gets in there, you can't remove it.

But you can dilute it. All your positive experiences – inspirational books, audiotapes and people – are like clear water. Pour enough of that into your glass and red will eventually become diluted to the point that you no longer can see it.

Each one of us chooses his or her self-talk. Positive self-talk can change the very *color* of our lives.

Protect yourself from negatives

Many times, even well intentioned people will try to "rain on your parade." These are the dream-stealers, the "naysayers", and the self-appointed critics, experts and name-callers. They always seem to know what's best for you.

Sometimes, even people who love us - and think they are protecting us - will say things that bring about self-doubt.

"You can't do that."

"You're no leader."

"You've never done anything like that before."

"Remember the last time you tried something?"

Very early on in starting our business, I decided we would involve some family and friends in our dream. They did not share our vision, and they said some very discouraging things. These comments came at exactly the wrong time. We needed someone to say, "you can do this. How can we help?"

Their negative comments were dangerous, but we still valued their opinion. It was a confusing time. We soon realized that our future success would require us to protect our attitude. We started being very careful about whom we allowed to influence us. Here are some of the questions we asked:

➤ Have they done what we want to do?

➤ Do they have the same information?

➤ Are their dreams the same or as big?

Sometimes, those closest to you will jeopardize your progress. Maybe they fear change. Maybe their goals and values are different. You must run your own race, and with a positive self-image, you will be sustained by your own belief that you have what it takes to make it.

Stay around those who will encourage and empower you along the way. You need to be the captain of your own ship. You need the courage to go deep inside yourself, grabbing hold of who you are and what you want. God does have a plan for each one of us. It's up to us to find it. Then, we must follow it to discover significance in our lives.

Find your area of excellence

As you attempt to build this positive and healthy self-image, it is possible to gain confidence by discovering one or two areas where you really excel. It is my experience that even if the skill is unrelated to your primary career, being good at something builds self-esteem.

I taught myself to play the guitar while I was in college. It was totally irrelevant to my engineering classes, but it didn't matter. I love music. I felt good about that achievement. That feeling translates into a foundation for a positive self-image.

When our youngest son, David, was growing up, Nancy and I encouraged him to pursue various activities where he could build his skills. He learned to play golf (a lot better than me), became a certified scuba diver, mastered snow skiing in the Rockies, and made the high-school tennis team. These skills give him a level of self-confidence that spills over into all other areas.

David experienced the process that leads to a healthy self-image. He struggled to develop his skills in each of these sports. He remembers how difficult it was. But now, he looks back at the experience and sees personal growth and self-confidence. He feels good about his accomplishments.

Our son Eric has mastered snow skiing as well, even though Nancy and I nearly need medical attention every time he heads up the mountain. He snorkels in Hawaii and the Caribbean. He plays billiards and chess. He speaks fluent Spanish.

He also has started a team sport in Atlanta called Power Soccer, where athletes in power wheelchairs can compete with others around the world. He raises money with his companions to offer aid and encouragement to those less fortunate than himself. His self-image is just fine.

Our daughter, Heather, is a talented businesswoman, an excellent mom, and has a sense of humor that could put most professionals out of business. And, by the way, our whole family has a much longer list of weaknesses, faults and failures. We all recognize them, but we choose to focus on those things that move us productively forward in life.

What can you do well? Are you a great cook? Can you sing? Do you have artistic talents? Are you a great coach, or cheerleader for people? Nancy feels that even if a young girl learned to prepare five or six great meals, she would be more confident and ready to believe she could learn and do other things.

Everyone has some area in which they excel. Find or learn one, build on that experience. And carry on into other areas of your life.

Borrow your self-image from others temporarily

Often, we are stuck in our own bad habits and self-limiting concepts. We know our weaknesses and hesitate to risk stepping into new or unknown areas. We need a little push from someone who sees better things for us. Speaking for myself, I've been blessed with a unique wife and partner for 34 years. From the beginning, Nancy was exactly what my self-image needed.

When we met in college, I was a small-thinking, rather negative and seriously analytical engineer. I was ambitious, but I wasn't utilizing all my special talents. I was mostly focused on what I observed as the strengths in others. I had developed a confidence in my abilities to master academics, but not in my abilities with people.

As an aeronautical engineer, in the advanced design group of McDonnell Douglas (now Boeing), I knew I could function in that narrow world of science and technology. My problem was that I had never succeeded in the world of business or leadership. I was still relatively young, and I was certainly no leader in high school or college. At Purdue University, all of my awards were for academic achievements – not for being the captain of the football team, or the president of the fraternity.

I soon realized the limitations of my career in aerospace. Nancy and I wanted far more out of life than my bosses were offering us. I had a crisis! I needed to believe I could succeed in a whole new area. I needed to be an entrepreneur, a leader, and even a speaker to large groups.

Gulp.

My secret weapon was – and still is – my wife, Nancy. Her optimism, decisiveness, and unsubstantiated confidence in me were amazing. Nancy's perceived weakness was that she was not much into details, and she didn't really want to talk to people, but she was a great dreamer. The details or facts didn't matter. She is an optimist and a person of action.

She would tell me over and over that she believed I could do anything. That included success in a people-oriented business. I thought she was crazy, and often found myself scrambling to keep up with the goals she had set for us. She chose a unique strategy. Even if my presentation was pathetic, she told me I had done well. She knew it was more important for me to believe in myself, rather than highlight my imperfections. As my confidence grew, so did my skill and effectiveness.

My wife was right—again!

Gradually, I began to change. I read dozens of books like *The Magic of Thinking Big*, *Think and Grow Rich*, and Dale Carnegie's *How to Win Friends and Influence People*. I made it a point to hang around people who contributed positively to my beliefs. I brushed myself off when I failed. As John Maxwell says, I kept failing forward. I was building a positive self-image by small steps of progress and improvement.

Here's how I built a better self-image:

- Continuing to pursue a dream when others were quitting all around me
- Continuing to get up when I fell down
- Making small progress when I feel the destructive power of doubt
- Realizing any little success meant progress
- Earning the respect of my peers in my industry through a series of small successes,

- Feeling satisfaction when I overcome a fear or solved a problem on my own
- Doing something well the first time I try it (or the second, or the third…)

You can't steer a parked car! Get in motion. Take baby steps. Why not?

A real self-image is the one you fight to earn on the inside. No one can take that from you. Nancy was my catalyst, my Professor Higgins from the movie, *My Fair Lady*. Then I read books, met other people and started experiencing small successes. I also developed my confidence with new self-talk.

Do you have someone who believes in you? Are you that person for someone else? Is someone looking to you right now for encouragement? We can be a powerful force in each other's lives as we all seek a positive, healthy self-image for lasting success.

10 Steps to a Positive Self-Image

1. Identify your strengths (and weaknesses)…don't seek perfection.
2. Look beyond yourself for a sense of value and purpose.
3. Don't be fooled by cultural or peer pressure - what really matters?
4. Discard the past, along with labels given to you by others.
5. Develop positive, constructive self-talk and encourage yourself whenever possible.
6. Protect your environment, you're effected by what you're exposed to – Garbage In, Garbage Out.
7. Feed your potential with books, tapes and healthy associations.
8. Build on all of your small successes.
9. Find your areas of excellence as a foundation of confidence.
10. Recognize and be thankful when you find a person who makes you believe in yourself

The Bible states so clearly, "As a man thinketh in his heart, so is he." A healthy, positive self-image is the key to achieving a life of significance and joy. It's hard to genuinely love and serve others if we don't have a love and respect for ourselves first. It's the foundation for all true success...a proper and positive view of our self.

My friend Charles "Tremendous" Jones has always said, "You will be the same today as you will be in five years, except for two things: the books you read and the people you meet." Let's begin anew today to establish that positive self-image you deserve.

You'll start to attract people with your healthy self-image. Because you feel so good about yourself, you won't be comparing yourself to others. You'll accept the occasional setbacks, but you won't get discouraged. You will keep moving forward.

The biggest dream-stealer I know is a poor self-image. You were designed for abundance, so let's begin the process of growing stronger and more confident every day.

You and your family deserve it!

3

Living A Principled-
Centered Life

By Dr. Ron Jenson

*"You never know a line is crooked
unless you have a straight one to put next to it."*
- Socrates

The average age of the world's greatest civilizations is been 200 years. These nations have progressed through the following sequence:

- from bondage to spiritual faith;
- from spiritual faith to great courage;
- from courage to liberty; from liberty to abundance;
- from abundance to selfishness;
- from selfishness to complacency;
- from complacency to apathy;
- from apathy to dependency;
- from dependency back into bondage.

As I shared these words with 17 Parliament Members in Uganda, I asked them where they saw their country. They turned around to and asked my associate and I where we saw the United States.

We both said, almost in unison, that we saw America at the level of complacency and apathy and sliding downhill fast... but with one caveat. We both saw 9/11/01 as a wake up call that had bumped many back to spiritual faith and great courage. Then, I said, what remains to be seen is whether we will maintain our courage or slide back into complacency and apathy and thereby move toward dependency and ultimately bondage.

Where do you think your culture (family, business and country) is on this progression? Where should it be? Where would you like it to be? What can you do about it?

I'd like to process with you what I believe is critical to a healthy culture—that is, a principle-centered lifestyle.

We are moving away from the underlying values that molded the free world, and the end result of this trend is clear from history—no values and the society falls apart. PERIOD. This is what is concerning all moral and ethical people in the world today.

Popular speaker and author Josh McDowell recently compared common school disciplinary problems from the 1940's and today. The 1940's punished gum chewing and running in the halls. Today the problems are rape, robbery and assault. Is this evidence of a society falling apart? Or is it just the result of population growth?

We've moved away from values rooted in universal principles. We see it in the educational realm and in business. Big Wall Street firms topple regularly. The moguls deal their lives and their wives away. Politicians change their stands on issues with as little thought as it takes them to come to one in the first place. Religious leaders, the ones we thought would embrace and model right values, embarrass us regularly. No area of our culture is free from the imprint of value-less thinking.

We see this in the headlines every day!

Syndicated columnist Cal Thomas in a book on ethics said the following:

> The Wall Street Journal *carried a story with the headline: "Ethics Are Nice, But They Can Be A Handicap, Some Executives Declare."*
>
> *The story reported on a survey conducted by the research firm McFeely Wackerle Jett.*

It asked 671 managers their views on the subject of ethics and business. The managers contended that ethics can impede a successful career and that more than half the executives they know would bend the rules to get ahead.

"I know of unethical acts at all levels of management," one fifty-year-old executive quoted in the study said. As his rationale for being unethical at times, he said, "I have to do it in order to survive."

For him, survival became the end, not honesty or truth. When such thinking becomes dominant in a culture, that culture is doomed.

The McFeely study also found that older executives generally think they are more principled than their younger counterparts. This is easily understandable given the sociological and moral upheaval younger men and women have gone through during the past twenty-five years.

The study quoted a fifty-nine-year-old vice-president at a Midwest company as saying, "Young M.B.A.'s and lawyers are taught opportunism, cleverness and cunning. Fairness and equity aren't given equal time or importance."

One of the best pieces of documentation on the decline in the American culture was the study entitled "The Day America Told the Truth—What People Really Think About Everything That Really Matters." This 270-page book written by James Patterson, Chairman of the J. Walter Thompson Co., and Peter Kim, Director of Research Services and Customer Behavior for this international advertising firm, clearly documents the kind of problems we're having in the area of ethics.

The book claims to be "the most massive in-depth survey of what Americans really believe that has ever been conducted." The book documents the impact of the lack of ethical standards. Backing up these observations the authors said: "Americans are making up their own rules and laws. We choose which laws of God we believe. There is absolutely no moral consensus in this country—as there was in the 50's and 60's."

Some of their findings were:

> *13 percent of the populace believes in all the biblical Ten Commandments.*

> *Nine out of ten Americans lie regularly.*

> *One-fifth of the nation's children had lost their virginity by age 13.*

> *For $10 million, seven percent of the people would kill a stranger.*

> *A third of all AIDS carriers have not communicated that truth to their spouses or lovers.*

So, what's the solution? A principle-centered life!

In this chapter I want to show you how you can identify and build absolute values into your life and business-absolute in every circumstance-that will give you stability and strength and, consequently, success and significance. For that, here is another acrostic to help you focus your thinking on the subject of morals and ethics:

V erify your own values

A rticulate your own ethical grid and philosophy of life

L earn the proper perspectives on issues

U npack right values through action

E valuate your growth

S hare these truths (your principles) with other people

Verify your own values

You need to determine just what value is directing your life. It's important from the outset to distinguish between principles and values. Basically, a value is your perception of where you're going in life. Your values may change, but principles do not. Your principles are the absolute. They are always true in every circumstance. Your values may change as your understanding of absolutes increases.

The point is that everyone is value-driven. A gang member is directed by his or her values. So are a mass murderer, a priest, and a dockworker. The issue is: Are their values based on right, universal principles or not? Universal principles produce the healthy roots of authentic success. False values not based on universal principles ultimately produce failure.

What is it, then, that you value? When this question is asked of people attending seminars, they usually try to articulate what they think they *should* value. But that's not the question! You should identify what you value *right now*. What values are reflective of your present lifestyle? Be honest! A rather rigorous evaluation here is critical; otherwise, you'll live in denial by not identifying the real root areas in your life that may need to change.

---

*It's hard to expect an empty bag
to stand up straight...*

If we don't have ethics or principles to give us substance and weight—if we're empty in the things that matter—we won't be the kind of models we want to be. Change begins with our value systems. And if the values of our society are declining, it's our fault.

Conduct an audit of your values by answering these questions:

➢ How do you spend your discretionary time?

➢ How do you spend your discretionary money?

➢ Who are your heroes?

➢ When you're alone, what do you think about most?

Your answers will demonstrate what your values are. Be honest and record what you are and do now, not what you think you ought to be and do. That will come later.

Try this exercise:

Do a one-week, authentic audit of your life. For an entire week, record how you spend your time, how you spend your discretionary money, whom you admire the most, and what you dream about.

Keep a daily log, and stop several times throughout the day to record your observations. Then, at the end of the week, go back and determine the things that you actually valued during that week. Next, ask yourself whether these are the values you want. Are you using your time, spending your money, focusing your dreams, and developing your role models the way you want to?

Articulate your universal principles

What is really important to you? Some people believe that the ethical thing to do is always "whatever will get me ahead." Take time right now to identify the things that are non-negotiable in your life—principles you will not violate, no matter what. Include principles that affect your work, your personal life, your family, your finances and your spirituality.

What is your personal philosophy or code of ethics? What is your family philosophy? What is your work philosophy?

Try these 10 MAXIMIZERS principles. Ask yourself how well you apply these 10 rules, both personally and professionally. Rate yourself on a scale of 1-10, with 10 being the highest score possible.

Make things happen - I take responsibility for life and develop consistent positive habits.

1............5............10

Achieve personal significance - I maximize my strengths and deal appropriately with my weaknesses.

1............5............10

X out the negatives - I embrace problems as positive opportunities.

1............5............10

Internalize right principles - I center my life on bedrock principles.

1............5............10

March to a mission - I passionately pursue my mission.

1............5............10

Integrate all of life - I keep all vital areas of my life in balance.

1............5............10

Zero in on caring for people - I put others first and honestly serve them.

1............5............10

Energize internally - I cultivate my character and spirit.

1............5............10

Realign rigorously - I keep adjusting to needs by focusing my positive emotions on resolving issues.

1............5............10

Stay the course - I - never, ever, ever quit.

1............5............10

The key is to dig your roots down to the bedrock of *truth* and let that source frame your values. If you do not articulate these philosophies, the culture will continually push you around. You must identify and promote the values you want to characterize yourself, values based on universal principles. If not, you can expect to spend the rest of your life as a slave to other people's values, your own dysfunctions, cultural pressures, or the values your own bad habits produce. The choice is yours.

Learn the right perspective on issues

Merely discovering what motivates your actions is not the end of this exercise. All of us need to continually look for *truth*; we need to make some actual determinations about right and wrong, about the ethical and unethical, about the moral, amoral, and immoral. And there *are* absolutes — universally accepted natural law principles that govern the universe and how people should live.

In *The Power of Ethical Management*, Ken Blanchard and Dr. Norman Vincent Peale simplify this search for truth with three questions to ask yourself at decisive times. I've added a fourth:

1. Is it legal? (Will I be violating either civil law or company policy?)

2. Is it balanced? (Is it fair to all concerned in the short-term as well as the long-term? Does it promote a win-win situation?)

3. How will it make me feel about myself? (Will it make me proud? Would I feel good if my decision were published in the newspaper, or if my family knew about it?)

4. Is it right? (Do I have any concerns inside as I consider my decision in light of what I understand to be right and wrong?)

Unpack right values through action

Now you're ready to start putting your values to work. It's one thing to develop an ethical grid of universal principles (truth) but quite another to work it out in your daily life.

Here's a strategy for doing this. Separate your life into three major areas: personal, family, and business. Choose for yourself a principle that you can put to work in each one of these areas such as *meet the needs of those around you!*

This is called "servant leadership." It is a code that urges you to build up other people in all possible ways. In the mid-1970s John Greenleaf, former director of management research at AT&T, wrote a landmark book entitled *Servant Leadership.*

Servant leadership, as Greenleaf describes it, focuses on your responsibility to build others, rather than on your rights and perks from being in a leadership position. It is the kind of leadership that says, <u>"I'm here to care for people and help them become successful."</u>

To live by this principle, you have to *burn this value of servant leadership into your mind.* You can do this by writing down a popular quotation or statement on servant leadership." <u>A servant leader is one who gets excited about making others more successful than themselves.</u>

Put these words on a 3x5- card and keep it before you during the day. Meditate on it four times. Think it through; chew on it; eat it up. Focus on that card as soon as you get up in the morning. Take a break at lunch and think about it. Reflect on it before dinner and then later, just before you go to sleep Program your mind with this thought.

Next, *think about ways you can a*, yourself questions about how you can your personal life. With whom do you Perhaps it's a gas station attendant, a wa call on the phone. How can you be a sour to these people?

Think through various situations that will come up in your daily activities and plan your servant-leadership attacks before they happen. You're bound to meet a grumpy waiter or waitress every now and then. What will you do?

In the arena of your family, your servant leadership may mean taking very deliberate time to be with your children, perhaps developing dates on a regular basis. These need to be planned, thought out, and activated. In the arena of your business, your servant leadership might be seen in the way you develop your employees or those for whom you have responsibility.

Evaluate your growth

To become truly ethically centered, spend time evaluating your efforts on a daily basis. Keep a journal on your growth for one week, taking time at the end of each day to ask the following questions related to your stated values:

- ✓ Did I schedule my principles and philosophy into my daily planner?
- ✓ Did I keep my schedule as I planned?
- ✓ How did I spend my idle time?
- ✓ Where did I spend my money?
- ✓ What did I daydream or dwell upon?
- ✓ Did my values inside match my values outside?

Or, establish a support group whose members will ask you regularly how you're doing. One reason Weight Watchers is such an effective weight-loss organizations is the accountability that personal trainers or coaches provide.

Whether your motivation is humiliation or being verbally rewarded for making positive headway, the impact of accountability and support works.

Share these truths with others

There are right ways and wrong ways to share what you're learning. Let me start with the wrong way.

Years ago I went through personal sales training. I thought I knew everything about how you relate to people in an open forum. And then one night I was at the Sea Fair Torch Light Parade in Seattle, Washington. I was walking along the parade route with a date. As we walked up and down (me basking in my new-found knowledge of sales and communications) I saw a young man walking on the street, ahead of the parade, passing out materials. I couldn't tell quite what he was giving people, but I was struck with how forthrightly he was forcing his materials on them without talking at all.

Being a newly enlightened salesman myself, I started to take offense with how he was communicating. After all, I'd just been trained that to sell effectively you must actually communicate. You must speak with people and solicit feedback. Therefore, since he was obviously doing it all wrong, I thought, that I would share these truths with him out of the kindness of my heart and the self-righteousness of my convictions.

So I went up to the gentleman, grabbed him by the shoulder, spun him around, looked at him right in the face, and said, "Excuse me, friend. I appreciate the fact that you have something here to communicate with people, but if you really want to be effective you'd communicate directly with them. Why don't you speak to people? It's more thoughtful, it's more sensitive, and it's more effective!"

You know what he said? Nothing but gibberish! He couldn't talk! He had lost his tongue.

I had demonstrated incredible audacity in speaking before I had the data, and it came back to bite me. That was a lesson I learned from life.

My word to you is, don't be pushy. Don't cram truth down people's throats. Be a friend, be a servant, meet their needs, and watch how they respond.

First, communicate *personally*. A rampant tendency exists among people today to want to air things publicly. This often occurs because we are insecure about addressing issues with people personally. Be brave and be direct in your personal interaction.

Second, communicate *positively*. It doesn't help to say to someone, "Here are twenty-five things you're doing wrong, and I only want to deal with one of them at this point." Instead, say, "There are many things in your life I wish I had in mine, but here's something I believe you may want to work on."

Third, communicate *practically*. There's nothing worse than identifying a generic problem in someone's life and not giving that person specifics. Once after speaking to a large crowd, a gentleman came up to the speaker and said, "I don't like you." She responded by saying, "I can understand that. You're just one of many. What don't you like about me?" He thought for a long time and said, "It's your personality."

Finally, communicate *patiently*. We often get upset when others push certain buttons in us. It is frustrating to see a developed habit become a pattern of impatience and anger. Learn to moderate this pattern over time, and continually work to alleviate it. Work at it all the time because impatience and anger stifle others' spirits. If we didn't continually work on being patient, we would lose credibility and impact. Learn to be patient when you communicate.

Whether you communicate with *reformative* or *formative* activity, you must aim to be a champion for values. Be a servant leader. Don't include yourself in the majority who are afraid to talk about truth, either because they haven't come to any conclusions or are afraid of repercussions.

Don't leave a legacy of relativity behind you. Leave a legacy of values, of truth, of rightness. It's your choice. Become committed to building bedrock, universal principles and embedding the roots of these principles *into your life.*

Take some action!

Values Clarification Exercise

1. Where do you spend your discretionary time?

2. How do you spend your discretionary money?

3. Who are your heroes?

4. When you're all alone, what do you think about the most?

5. What do the answers to these questions tell you about your values? Are they the same values you thought you lived by?

Principle development

1. What are the principles with which you want to form the map for your life? Begin to write these down. Place them prominently before you and begin to build them into your life as your code of conduct and organizing principles.

2. List at least one other person with whom you can form a support group to help you flesh out your values and walk your talk.

4

Identify Your What & Why -

By Hal Gooch

I wish you could have met me thirty years ago. I was a furniture worker in Thomasville, North Carolina. I was painfully shy, and filled with overwhelming feelings of inferiority. I looked at my feet when I spoke to people.

I've got a question for you—WHAT?

And WHY?

WHAT do you want out of life?

WHY are you working in your current profession, doing the things that you're doing with your life?

I don't know what your WHAT or WHY is, but I bet I could find out. If I had the chance to talk to you right now, I'd ask you some questions. Pretty soon, I'd figure out what motivates you.

Since I'm not there to ask the questions, you'll have to do it yourself.

WHAT do you want out of life? WHY do you want it?

Thirty years ago, making furniture in Thomasville, North Carolina, I realized I wanted more out of life. I didn't quite know HOW I would do it, but I knew WHAT and WHY.

Don't worry about HOW. Concentrate on your WHAT and WHY. Unless your WHAT and WHY are always bigger than your HOW, you'll probably be discouraged, disoriented and eventually unsuccessful. Your WHAT and WHY are that crucial to this process.

Dream big

To develop a huge WHAT and WHY, you need to start dreaming. You need to start dreaming BIG.

Thomas Edison was one of history's most powerful dreamers. He applied for 1,093 patents in his lifetime, the most ever granted one person. Edison patented the phonograph, incandescent electric lamp, motion-picture projector and carbon telephone transmitter.

Imagine life today without some of Edison's inventions. We can all be Edison's. We just need the right kind of dreams.

We can do anything if we dream BIG enough. It all starts in our minds. The first step is to know exactly what you want. What's your goal? What's your desire?

If you're not clear about this, write it down. If necessary, rewrite it, so the words express precisely what you want to achieve.

Here's what you're doing – you're "imagining as possible." That's Webster's definition, and I really like it. The mind is a very powerful force. If the dream is BIG enough, the facts don't count.

Let me say that again – if the dream is BIG enough, the facts don't count. Conventional wisdom is irrelevant.

What if Helen Keller had listened to conventional wisdom? Blind, mute and deaf from infancy, she overcame these immense barriers to learn how to read, write and speak. Before her death in 1968 at 88 years of age, she became admired around the world for her speeches, writing, and life.

What if Walt Disney had listened to his critics? He faced disbelief and bankruptcy when he began developing his vision. Today, the memory of the man who gave the world Mickey Mouse, Donald Duck, and Disney World stands as a lasting memory to his phrase, "all our dreams can come true, if we have the courage to pursue them."

We all hear negative voices. Helen Keller heard them. Walt Disney heard them, too. But they didn't listen. All the negatives didn't distract them.

You won't listen, either, because you're going to fill your mind with positives. These positive voices will allow you to break free. You'll be better equipped to forge your own successful life.

Are you ready to get started?

1. **Take total responsibility for what you've been, what you are and what you will become.** Take responsibility NOW!! Don't spend your life blaming yourself or others. Blaming doesn't help anybody. You can only be successful and happy when you start taking responsibility for yourself.

2. **Develop your own dreams.** Others, often well-meaning family and friends, sometimes influence you to do what they want – their dreams. Only you know what you're capable of doing. You have to set your own self-expectations if you want to be the best YOU.

3. **Become obsessed with learning.** No matter where you are, you can take night courses at a local community college or nearby university. In today's video, DVD and cassette era, anyone can take advantage of the abundant array of educational and motivational opportunities. Thousands of these tools beckon you to open the doors to your future.

4. **Seek our mentors and colleagues who will help bring out your best in the future.** If you want to be great, professionally and personally, associate yourself with the finest and best people. Let me see who your friends and associates are, and I can predict who you will become. Choose your friends and mentors very carefully.

Being the best you!

Before you decide what you want to be, you must figure out where you are right now. What makes you tick? What do you need to change before you can achieve more in life?

King Solomon once wrote, "Wisdom is the principal thing; therefore, get wisdom. And in all your getting, get understanding." Before you can understand others, you must learn to understand yourself better.

What are your values? These beliefs provide a focus for your life. People without a clarified value system tend to look only at results that can be easily measured – a college degree, shooting a 72 in golf, an amount in the bank. Values-based people, by contrast, seem to express their core beliefs by measuring themselves against themselves, by doing their best.

So, how do you clarify your values? Do a personal inventory of your priorities in life, and the talents you'll use to achieve those goals.

Look into the future and see yourself in 10 years.

- ✓ Where will you be living?
- ✓ What will you be doing?
- ✓ What assets will you own?
- ✓ Will you be happy?

Here's the most important part of the inventory. Complete the following sentence: More than anything, I want

_____.

Now that you've answered, let me ask the following question: **Just how much do you want it?**

Seeking to know yourself – what you truly value and really want – must become an all-consuming, driving mission. It's that important!

From years of dreaming and planning with thousands of small-business people, I have come to the conclusion that a definition of success must come from within – deep inside. And the desire to reach it must come from inside as well. Both the dream and desire will spring from our values. The sooner we know them and understand them, the sooner our real journey can begin.

What do you want to be? Before you can answer, you must figure out:

➢ Where are you right now?

➢ What makes you tick?

➢ What do you need to change before you can achieve more in life?

➢ How can you turn your weaknesses into strengths?

You see, having strong values is no accident. Success is no accident. Failure is no accident. Success and failure are the result of your values, your choices and your actions.

The plan

During World War I, German submarines were causing considerable concern for the Americans. During a gathering, cowboy satirist Will Rogers was asked, "What would you do about the subs if you were president?"

"That's easy," the humorist replied. *"I'd drain the Atlantic Ocean dry, and then you could see all of those machines and blow 'em up."*

"How in the world could you drain the ocean dry?" an onlooker asked incredulously.

"Look," Rogers said. *"I came up with the idea. Now, you smart guys figure out how to get it done."*

In this unforgettable exchange, Will Rogers described the plight of so many big dreams (and would-be dreamers). Coming up with ideas is easy. Putting together an action plan is the hard part.

You must break your dreams apart – into pieces small enough to conquer one by one. By turning your dreams into achievable goals, you allow your vision to empower your dreams, and your dreams to fuel your goals.

Here's how:

1. **Your goals must be achievable**. A goal is not some vague "pie-in-the-sky" pipe dream or absurd fantasy. A good goal is one that causes you to stretch all your abilities, but one you're reasonably confidant you can reach. Only you know the difference between a dream and a fantasy. You'll need three kinds of goals:

   - Long-range goals covering several years, but usually not more than 10.

   - Intermediate goals, breaking down long-range goals into annual or semi-annual steps.

   - Short-range goals, breaking down intermediate goals into monthly or weekly steps.

   The secret to setting goals is to develop a system to motivate yourself and keep yourself accountable. That will prevent you from getting discouraged, and lack the persistence to keep piercing the walls of resistance. Keep those long-range goals out there to keep you from being frustrated by short-range failures.

2. **Your goals must be worthwhile**. You must believe your goals have value. Find goals that make you enthusiastic. The key to all self-discipline is desire. The more you want something, the easier self-discipline becomes.

3. **Your goals should be clear-cut**. The more specific the goal, the better your chances of reaching it.

4. **Your goals need a timetable**. You must hold yourself accountable to deadlines. Unless you write your goals and timetables, you probably aren't serious about reaching them.

   What happens if you don't fulfill your goals? I remember one backwoods preacher who used to say, "It's better to shoot for the moon and hit the picket fence than to aim for the fence and hit the ground!" Give it your best shot, and you will always have the inner satisfaction of knowing that you tried.

What about your plan of action?

Take a few moments and write a statement about what your life could be like in five years, providing you continue living as you are right now. Remember to cover all the areas of life that are important to you.

Then, write a sentence or two detailing the changes you would like to make in your life during the next five years, in each of the important areas.

Finally, what are the key strategies you will need to make those changes?

Your dreams are like riding through a prosperous neighborhood and trying to imagine living in one of those beautiful houses. Setting goals is like picking out one of those homes. But in addition to having dreams and goals, you must also develop a concrete plan to make your aspirations come true. You have to be a practical dreamer.

Now, what do you want to do in the next five years? How are you going to reach those goals? What is your action plan?

Be flexible

I learned this quote many years ago:

"Success if not the reverse of failure; it is the scorn of failure. Always dare to fail; never fail to dare."

The only thing you can control is how you motivate yourself as you face both good and bad circumstances.

1. **A positive day starts the night before**, so spend some time each night reflecting on the good things that happened during your day.

2. **Begin each day positively**. The most important hour in each day is often the first hour you are awake. Starting out the day on a positive note sets a tone for being able to handle everything that happens.

3. **Keep goals constantly in front of you.** Visualize yourself reaching your goals and replay that mental picture. No matter what arises, you will be able to keep your sense of direction.

4. **Keep reminding yourself why you want to succeed**. One millionaire has been asked many times why he succeeded, when his childhood friends never made it. His simple answer? "I guess I just had more reasons to get rich than they did."

5. **Be flexible, even in the area of criticism**. Learn what you can from feedback of friends, business associates - and certainly, the competition. Change what you should.

Anyone who has ever succeeded in anything has felt the stinging darts from jealous people. The only way to avoid criticism is to say nothing, do nothing and be nothing!

The greatest question is not, "Will I keep getting knocked down?"

Here's the greatest question: "Will I keep getting up?"

What we do with our mistakes is the one thing that determines what we get out of life. Never allow yourself to stay wallowed in your misery. Say to yourself, "How can I make something good come out of this?"

Most people don't quit on life deliberately, but they give up their vision one piece at a time when they run into barriers or detours. Determine over and over what success means to you, then do whatever is necessary to make changes, so you can achieve your dreams.

Building your team

I live within an hour of Duke University, North Carolina State and the University of North Carolina. Any basketball fan will understand the excitement you feel when the Blue Devils, Wolfpack or Tarheels run onto the court.

The roar shakes you to the core. Even the most restrained people get caught up in such contagious, exhilarating moments. When national rankings or conference championships are on the line, the intensity is unbelievable. The excitement ignites a fire that spreads throughout the fans, and no words can adequately describe how it feels.

While individual players may get the headlines, it takes teams to win games. Teamwork, quite simply, is vital. It's true in basketball. It's true in this business, as well.

The late J. Paul Getty, one of the richest men in history, once said, "If you help enough people get what they want, you will automatically get what you want."

But getting people to work with you is one of the toughest character-building exercises you will ever experience. As J. Paul Getty suggested, you can't focus on what YOU want. You must focus on what each member of your team wants.

How do you figure that out? By asking questions.

When you ask questions, you get beneath the surface, discovering and revealing what's going on inside each person. You'll make each team member feel important, as he or she expresses individual wants and needs. You will involve him or her in the overall process.

Sounds simple, but good questions must be prepared in advance. Mentors and co-workers can tell you what works for them. They'll tell you that open-ended questions – ones that don't allow a "yes" or "no" answer – are best. Open-ended questions allow others to tell you how they feel, what they want and what they think.

You don't want to offend anyone with questions that are too personal or intimidating. Start with broad inquiries, with questions that are easy to answer. Studies show most people like to agree, rather than assert themselves and disagree. Make it easy for people to react positively.

Then, be quiet. Listen.

You can easily talk too much, so consciously reduce your talking time. So ask questions that allow the other person to do the talking. Try some of these:

-   "Tell me more…"
-   "What do you mean…?"
-   "How will you…?"
-   "If you were in my shoes, what would you…?
-   "What do you think about…?"
-   "How can I find out about…?"

Maybe you're asking all the right questions, but you're seeing some bad body language – signs of discomfort or disagreement. Change your approach and reset the stage. If the nonverbal communication is extremely negative, you may find the only way out is to get back with the other person on another day.

Always remember to listen carefully to the other person's complete comment or question before you talk. By reacting too quickly, you can actually destroy any rapport or credibility you have established.

The only way you can help others get what they want is to discover and uncover what is important to them. Do that by asking questions.

Motivating others

People will generally work harder for emotional benefits and recognition than they will for monetary reward. They're naturally drawn to be part of something worthwhile and exciting.

Human resource professionals insist that as much as 90 percent of the things we do in life are fueled by a desire to feel important.

Here's how to motivate your team:

- ✓ Do simple favors for others
- ✓ Learn and use their names
- ✓ Be aware of people, and value them
- ✓ Encourage communication and approachability
- ✓ Be kind and forgiving toward others
- ✓ Allow people to work through their own challenges
- ✓ Surprise people

Says Renn Zaphiropoulos, president of the Versatec Corporation, "When you give someone a check, don't mail it. Have a celebration."

A secret to your success is to develop your team's cohesiveness. Develop the ability to believe in others and reward them. What gets rewarded gets done.

I have spent most of my adult lifetime studying people. Virtually every person who is able to achieve and sustain great success in life is a great team-builder. The secret to great team building can often be reduced to one word: TRUST.

So, if you want to achieve much, build powerful teams. To do that, build trust. To build trust, you must develop these three trust-builders:

- ➤ HONESTY
- ➤ INTEGRITY
- ➤ COURAGE.

Honesty is pretty much self-explanatory, but let me give you some ideas about integrity and courage. Integrity means doing what's right, no matter what. Courage means holding on, when everybody else is telling you to quit. Honesty, integrity and courage are the foundations of leadership; the foundations you'll need to motivate others.

These traits will help you develop consistency, another necessary component of success. You should strive to be consistently better than anyone else in the following areas:

- Do more homework and preparation
- Learn more
- Do more exercise, and stay in the best physical shape possible
- Drive the cleanest car, and wear the cleanest, best-pressed clothes
- Be the most organized
- Be memorable

When I want you to be memorable, I'm not encouraging you to be tacky or eccentric. But you must look the part you want to play. Within 30 seconds of walking into a room where no one knows you, people will make several judgments about you, based on how you look, talk and act.

So stand up straight, have a firm handshake and make good eye contact. Don't overdo it – don't be a stiff with a crushing grip and an icy stare. But strive to present a good appearance, because it suggests the presence of self-confidence.

How do you sound? If your voice isn't as warm or effective as you'd like, seek the assistance of a good vocal coach. Take a public speaking course at a local college. Join Toastmasters. Whatever you do, learn to make the best of your voice.

The best businessmen and women have a talent for making an impact on the opinions and actions of others –an influence so subtle that it may go unnoticed at first.

The customer

Here's where you can really stand out. How many times do you remember when anyone in the marketplace treated you as if you were royalty? Enough said!

Here is your challenge: In the age of carelessness and shoddy work, can you go the "extra mile" and do the things no one else seems willing to do? Service is key to your business. Whatever you do, in terms of customer care, will make you stand out from the competition.

But that message has to get through to your team. When leaders don't motivate well, teams almost always fail. Ask yourself these questions:

- What are you motivating people toward?
- Are your team members expected to do things for which they've never been prepared?
- Do you lack the courage or conviction to sell your ideas to others?
- Do you lack the willingness or ability to support others?

You must work to overcome your own failures, while seeking to help your team members face their challenges. This is the essence of teamwork and leadership. Here are some principles for fostering strong team spirit:

1. **Build ownership among the entire team**, so people see the organization's purpose as an extension of their own personal purposes. That way, they'll assume responsibility for the company's success.

2. **Ask, don't tell**. When you ask questions, you encourage creativity, reduce resistance and inspire others.

3. **Foster innovation throughout the organization**. Keep saying, "Let's find a better way to do this – together."

4. **Have fun**. Sure, it's work. But you have to find a way to make it interesting, and, yes, even fun.

Community is the key. People can be united by e-mail, audiotapes, programs, conventions, incentive programs, team meetings and televised get-togethers. All of these work well.

The next level

Before I turn you loose, I have some final words of advice. As you build your business, don't forget to look outside of your organization for help. There is an old Chinese proverb: "When the student is ready, the teacher appears." I have found that each time I was ready for the next challenge, a mentor appeared.

Mentors can help new managers learn important skills. They can model ways to attack problems and develop solutions. They can help you build a better team, by emphasizing skill and behavior. But you have to find them, so keep your ears open. If you want to learn from leaders, seek to be in the midst of leaders.

I've learned one of life's greatest secrets, and it's really quite simple: Those small, supposedly insignificant differences between you and your competitors can mean everything. It's attention to detail – a slight edge.

Look at the sports world. Races, including the Kentucky Derby and NASCAR events, have been determined by inches. The greatest golf tournaments come down to one final putt during a sudden-death ending.

In business, you can join that select group of high achievers by becoming a master at image, preparation and confidence. It all begins by making a good first impression.

Of course, there is always an element of risk. In fact, if you take the risk out of life, you take out the opportunity. The secret is calculating and controlling the amount of risk as you take the next step.

But take a chance. Time after time, in business and consulting, I have found that as you step out to reach for your dreams, the resources become available. You will realize the greatest gift in life is not things, but the ability to use your experience and the wisdom of others to make the most of your opportunities.

Be persistent. You see, life does not always grant your first dream, or your second or even your hundredth. Nobody, but nobody wins every skirmish, or goes through life unscathed. Success and barriers are almost always linked. I don't know anyone who has achieved very much without suffering from bad judgment, defeats and failures – yet came back stronger than before.

Every life has both victories and losses. Stand apart from both and examine why each occurred to you. You show your true character in these situations, at either end of the spectrum. That's what true freedom is – doing your best and accepting the results.

Write down what kind of person you want to be. Invest time to become that person. Choose your roads carefully. Travel with patience, and you will discover how wonderful the journey can be. You will turn your dreams into reality and touch the lives of thousands of others.

Build and maintain an always positive attitude in your business!

5

Visualize The Finish Line

By Beverly Sallee

"Choose me, choose me!

"Please choose me!"

These words ring in my ears from elementary school. We all remember choosing teams – and we all remember not wanting to be the last one chosen.

"Do I have to choose her?" the captain would say.

For many of us, those are painful words. We were not the first to be chosen. I was usually one of the last, because I was a better musician than athlete. Throughout my school career I was the tallest girl in my class. Sometimes they didn't want a tall girl, especially for baseball or track. I wanted to be accepted at such a deep level, that I turned to academics and music to gain my recognition.

I visualized myself being the captain of the spelling team, the reading team or the math team – and I was able to choose others for a change. After some months of work, it actually happened. Then, we would move to a new town and I would start over at a new school.

My father was in the Army and later worked for the Immigration and Naturalization Service and the Border Patrol. He'd get transferred, and the cycle continued and I'd have to start all over again – a new school, a new challenge.

At night, I was terrified to have the lights turned out and the door closed at bedtime. My sister was younger, but she wasn't afraid at all. This was very embarrassing, so I said nothing. I'd just shut my eyes tight and began to visualize beautiful things to take my mind off the fear. I imagined myself in glamorous clothes with high heels, gloves and a big hat strolling through an art gallery or a hotel lobby, being admired by everyone. The feeling of being accepted was so important.

In the middle of my father's career, he decided he wanted to try farming. He had been raised on a farm and determined it was time for his children to experience a similar lifestyle to his. My sister and I were in our early teens and were not excited about this new direction.

Regardless of our misgivings we moved to a very small town in east Texas and my father set up a large dairy farm. I wasn't too eager to spend my time with cows. I had been a city girl, and thought I had better things to do than milk every morning and evening.

Gradually, I realized what my father wanted to teach me. I saw my parents' good attitude and work ethic, and I began to see the value of what they were doing. It was their dream and they were living it out. My sister and I gradually began to participate. We soon adjusted to the small-town life and began to enjoy it.

We made lots of friends and participated in all the activities of a small-town high school. Now, as I look back, I realize many of my values were set at that time. The experience of my parents adjusting to new circumstances - going through the good and bad times - helped me handle adversity as an adult.

My mother became very ill and was in the hospital for several weeks. At the same time, wholesale prices for milk dropped drastically. The prices were so low that my father decided to sell out and move. I was only 14, but I obtained a driver's license and drove our family car several hundred miles to a new city. I followed my father, as he drove a big truck with all our possessions inside.

We began a new life in that city. Once again, we adjusted to our new setting and prospered. Many times in my adult life, I have looked back to that experience. Although it was difficult at the time, I gained strength from it. Remembering those events, visualizing them in my mind's eye, has given me courage to go through other difficult things.

This is a unique form of visualization that gives sight to the end result...the finish line. I find it valuable, to recall past experiences in a visual sense to assure that I not repeat former mistakes. By remembering our trials and triumphs we acquire the ability to gain new strength and direction.

Piano lessons

I used this form of visualization in another area of my life. I started taking piano lessons when I was nine years old. As I excelled, I began to visualize playing on stage before large audiences. My first time was anything but successful. I was in high school and several of us were asked to go to the local Army base and entertain wounded soldiers.

I thought it would be like the Bob Hope shows overseas. One girl performed a beautiful dance, another sang a popular song and I was to play a classical piece on the piano. They were not in the mood for anything serious. I was so mortified that I tried to turn it into a jazz piece. I'm sure Mozart would have been deeply offended at my rendition.

However, with more practice and maturity, I began to lose my fear of playing in public and live my dream of playing before an audience. I lost my fear of making mistakes. This is the key to delivering your best performance – in music or any other activity. Accepting blunders, laughing at them, and relating them to others is great therapy. Here's the way I get ready to perform:

- ✓ Be as well-prepared as possible
- ✓ Say a little prayer
- ✓ Forgive myself in advance
- ✓ Picture the audience smiling and applauding

You will find this formula gives you a lot more pride and confidence in your presentations.

You have to start small, not at Carnegie Hall. When I first began to perform, my piano pieces were short. The audiences were small. Gradually, the pieces were longer and the audiences bigger.

The largest audience I ever had was in an outdoor arena in Mexico City. There were 55,000 people in attendance. When I look back on that performance, I don't remember being afraid. It takes years of practice, but it can be done.

I remember performing for a ladies luncheon in Oregon. There were about 300 women enjoying a lovely outing overlooking the majestic northwest scenery. Normally, I would not eat before playing and singing. But on this day, there was a Hawaiian luau. Everything looked so delicious.

I ate much more than I should have. After the luncheon, it was my turn to perform. As I played the introduction and took my first breath, nothing came out of my mouth, not a single note. I stopped and said, "excuse me, ladies, I have to unzip my skirt or I won't be able to sing a note." Of course they all laughed, I relaxed and was able to sing the song.

Similar to my musical performance, I was getting up to speak before an audience when nonchalantly I passed by a book display. The books were on a revolving wire rack. The wire caught on my sleeve, and the fabric of my blouse promptly started unraveling.

Nothing to do, but make a joke of it. I simply plunged ahead - with a drooping sleeve. I had learned that nothing is a big deal, unless we allow it to happen. It helps me move forward and not be paralyzed by failure.

No one succeeds all the time. Sometimes, your presentation is going to unravel – along with your sleeve.

Based on my experiences I have learned not to visualize failure. I visualize success. Before I present a business plan or do a seminar, I visualize how the meeting will go. Sometimes, I will remind myself it couldn't be any worse than some of the unsuccessful meetings I've experienced.

✓ Here's a format for visualization:

- Quickly remember unpleasant experiences
- Laugh at yourself
- Plan your upcoming performance

Even though there will be last-minute changes, your visualization will help you adjust as you see the actual set-up.

✓ Here is a formula for making your best presentation:

- Have a strategy
- Rehearse your performance
- Control the situation
- Be satisfied with the results

Remember, things will go wrong – at exactly the wrong time. I once sang at an event called the Bach Festival. It was a big performance for me, and I was nervous. Just before I went on stage, I ran to the ladies room.

I was carrying my sheet music. Somehow, I dropped it – into the water. By the time I pulled it out, the music was soaked. Just then, I heard the bells, signaling that the performance was about to begin. I shook off as much water as I could, and went on stage with dripping music.

As they say, "The show must go on."

And it does – ready or not. We have the choice to prepare for the proper outcome.

As an adult, my first full-time job was as a music teacher. I loved it, but I also loved to travel. As a music teacher, I didn't have much money. But I had time.

So I taught myself a very important lesson in delayed gratification.

Delayed gratification

Each year, I would find the place where I wanted to spend my summer months. Then, I'd save every dime I could. While I was saving, I'd send away for brochures on the region. I checked out movies, thought about my vacation - anything to keep visualizing the actual experience. Hawaii, Scandinavia, Mexico, Europe, South America, and South Africa – those were my destinations.

The sacrifices necessary to save money weren't so hard. I cooked at home, rather than going out to eat. I stayed home and read books, rather than spending money on a movie.

I could see my goal getting closer all the time. Marking off the days on the calendar was an exciting event. That didn't cost me anything, either!

This experience was invaluable when I went into business for myself. Determining how much time I would spend developing my business was no different than all those hours I had practiced my music. It was simply a matter of learning to focus on the purpose. Once that was established, the rest was just follow-through.

Henrietta Mears said, "There are three parts to travel; anticipation, participation, and reflection. Often the participation is the least enjoyable." I agree.

I would spend months anticipating the trip, visualizing each place and learning about it. When I actually went, I always experienced some setbacks - the weather might be bad, the time went by too quickly, or I didn't have enough money.

But you can reflect on your vacation for the rest of your life. You have pictures, souvenirs and memories.

I think these three principles apply in other areas of our lives. It certainly applied in my business. I set aside the time to develop the business. I planned, dreamed and focused on the results I would achieve.

The big day arrived and I achieved the recognition I desired, it was fulfilling. I had my moment of fame, but then, it was over. Still, I have the rest of my life to remember and reflect on all that I had accomplished:

- Triumph Over Obstacles
- Victory Over Pain
- Enjoyment
- Satisfaction
- Residual Income

Because of these principles it is very important to instantly make another goal and start the same process again. Do not fall into the trap that catches many people – once they finish their education, they often times become depressed. They have realized the goal of getting a degree, but now, they feel aimless. They need to re-establish what they want to accomplish and set some new long-range goals.

Once I achieved my major business goal, I began to focus on giving scholarships to young musicians. I've found that goals involving charities have roots in the lives of the donors. I had tried many times to get scholarships, so I could attend graduate school. I had the goal, but I was in the wrong field. They were giving scholarships for science, not for music.

This became my mission – to offer music scholarships to graduate students. For fifteen years, I have donated multiple scholarships for students every year to come to the United States to study. I also send students abroad to participate in international music festivals. These are all coordinated through the Oregon Bach Festival and the Bachakademie in Germany.

I also enjoy doing leadership training in Third World countries to help develop leadership skills. So many people come to the United States for a college education, but they never return to their native countries. My goal is to help develop business overseas, to change their way of life. I can help develop leaders who set new standards in their native countries.

It has always been important for me to set goals. I put them into the following categories:

- ➢ Daily Goals
- ➢ Weekly Goals
- ➢ Monthly Goals
- ➢ Yearly Goals
- ➢ Long-Term Goals

In my journal, I record my activities every day. I also have a daily calendar, to jot down those activities that need to be done, next to my appointments. Every night, I see what I accomplished and write down an agenda for the next day

At the end of the month, I evaluate what I accomplished in the last four weeks. At the end of the year, I look back. It's always amazing to me when I see how many have come true. All it takes is writing them down, and putting the work habits in place to achieve them.

My favorite saying is, "If it is to be, it's up to me."

It is natural to get distracted, diverted, and discouraged. One of the best ways to counteract that is to stay plugged in to your goal. Do this by reading and listening to messages of those people who have achieved success in your field. It gives you the ability to associate with them and adopt similar processes.

This is how I kept visualizing success. I kept going to seminars, listening to the speaker and picturing myself at the podium. This was a powerful incentive. Think about what it is like when you go to a movie. What is on the screen becomes reality for a short time, if you let yourself become absorbed by the experience.

You might see yourself in the setting of the movie, or as the main character in the story. You can make a movie out of your life. You can put yourself on the big screen, constantly visualizing your dream. When you set a goal like this, watch how many things in your life come together to make it a reality.

Suddenly, you see articles everywhere - in magazines, newspapers and books - about things you can use to help achieve your dream. Before understanding the power of visualization you might not have noticed.

Here's a short checklist of steps you can take:

- ✓ Listening to tapes of people who are successful
- ✓ Emulating their style or voice inflection until it becomes a daily habit
- ✓ Reading self-improvement books and biographies of successful people every night

These steps will give you hope and direction to achieve your goals too. It has been differentiating factor for me throughout my career.

In my business, it is my role to cast vision. As I go into a developing country to set up operations, it is imperative that I visualize what these people can do to overcome their difficult circumstances. At first, a visit outside the United States can be a shocking experience. You walk in the shoes of what other people face on a daily basis. I recommend this experience to all Americans. It will give you a perspective on this world that will serve you well throughout your life.

Starting a business in Hungary was my first experience in an eastern European market. One afternoon, I drove with several local friends out to a school in the countryside, about two hours from Budapest. About fifty people gathered to learn about the chance to experience owning their own business. They were anxious to see if this really was an opportunity to give them hope and direction for the future.

Standing in front of them, with interpreters for Hungarian and Polish, I painted dreams for them. Writing on a small black slate board with a tiny piece of chalk, I showed them how they could make a difference for many others.

Several years ago, I started my business in India. What a vast land, with over a billion people. The opportunities are great, but so are the obstacles. I kept reassuring them if they would follow a few simple principles, they could begin to see their dreams come true.

Many phone calls, e-mails, and visits brought the vision of creating significant opportunities for many in Third World families into reality. It has been such a wonderful journey, establishing markets with a great support organization called Network 21. Jim and Nancy Dornan, the founders of Network 21, are people of character, integrity and great vision. They have inspired thousands to think bigger all the time.

Dealing with setbacks

When I was teaching high school, there was a group of teachers that rode motorcycles in the desert during school holidays. I don't like motorcycles, but everyone else was doing it.

"Come on, Beverly," they said.

Motorcycles frightened me, so I was reluctant to don the leather coat and ride into the sunset. But I thought I needed to ride, simply to be accepted.

Big mistake.

On one particular weekend, we visited Anza-Borrego desert in California. One of my friends was baby-sitting my four-month old daughter back at camp. I had been on a long ride and was so glad it was finally over. I was riding in deep sand, but I got careless. I violated two important rules for this type of riding – don't let off the gas and don't turn quickly.

The bike flipped over. My leg was under it.

I knew immediately it was broken. It took seven hours to get me to a hospital, and I was in pain the whole time.

"It looks like she hit a brick wall," said the orthopedic surgeon when he looked at the x-rays. For a week, the doctors discussed whether they should operate to try to put it back together. Many prayers later, they decided to put my leg in a cast and send me home.

I was in a body cast for months. Finally, the doctor took it off to see if I could put any weight on my leg.

Each day, I looked out the window and saw people walking across the street. "Do they appreciate just walking across the street?" I wondered. I certainly did not take it for granted now. Each day, I could use the crutches to get in a standing position and press my foot on a bathroom scale. But I could only put five pounds of weight on my leg – for just ten minutes.

Each week, I could increase the pressure by five pounds, until I reached my body weight. Every day, I struggled to go through this exercise. But I visualized myself walking again. I saw myself playing the organ again - using both feet on the pedals.

Day after day, I sat up in bed and tried to care for my little girl. Often I would pull myself up into the wheelchair and take her on my lap. Off we'd go to the bathroom for a bath. Washing her became a monumental task. Without help from my husband and my friends, this would have been impossible.

After three months, I was able to take my first steps. On that same day, my daughter took her first steps. What a day of celebration! I am still grateful I can walk and live a normal life. I worked hard to get back what I had lost.

Many times, we don't go ahead with our goals and dreams because we are not sure it is worth the struggle. But I knew how much I wanted to walk again. Visualization is powerful in this area. Of course, if you do not push through you will not know what you could have achieved. But if you do not put your dreams in front of you every day, they have no hope of becoming real for you.

Dr. Ron Jenson's book, *Achieving Authentic Success™*, has some very practical principles for making our lives work. I first met Dr. Jenson in India, where he was conducting leadership training. I was struck by the acceptance of the principles he was teaching. We went on to other countries in Europe, and his teachings were equally appreciated.

Dr. Jenson has a comparison of the value of work in the "time-honored view and the growing view," as he calls it. He suggests that people once thought of work as a vocation or calling. Now, it is merely an occupation.

It used to be a place that reflected proper values. Now it is a place to get what you want.

It used to be a place that focused on giving. Now, the focus is on receiving.

In my family there was a strong work ethic. My grandparents were farmers, and they worked long hours every day. So did all the children. My parents usually worked two jobs. While my mother raised us, she took on work that could fit into the family schedule. My sister and I helped with the work each day after school. We learned how to budget time for work and play.

Aunt Ethel

My first mentor in business was my Aunt Ethel. She was my mother's older sister and had built a multi-million dollar dress design company, specializing in girls' dresses. She sold her dresses in the New York and Dallas markets for more than 40 years. With no experience or schooling at all, she designed one dress and sold it to a neighbor for her little girl. Gradually, other neighbors began to buy dresses she had designed. This was during the Depression, so money was scarce.

She said when she looked at the cloth, she could see the finished product. Her strong sense of imagination and her ability to visualize the end result enabled her to create exquisite dresses. She overcame sorrow in her own life to achieve her dreams. She lost two of her children. Her husband lost his job and the Depression enveloped their lives. Through it all, she found enough hope to go on and build an empire. Out of her discouraging circumstances, she triumphed.

She would often call and remind me, "Beverly, we are the kind of women that keep the bread lines short in this country."

This is a very strong part of visualization - having someone else believe in you when you don't believe in yourself. That can really change things. Aunt Ethel did that for me.

She had a unique philosophy. She called it The Secret of Making Money - GO TO WORK - go to work.

- If you are poor...work.
- If your health is threatened...work.
- If disappointments come...work.
- If you are rich, continue working.
- If faith falters and reason fails...work.
- If dreams are shattered and hope seems dead... work.
- If sorrow overwhelms you and loved ones are untrue...work.
- If you are burdened with seemingly unfair responsibilities...work.
- If you are happy, keep right on working.

Idleness gives room for doubt and fear. No matter what ails you, work. Work as if your life is in peril, for it is.

As my business grew internationally, I would send her cards from all over the world. Invariably when I got home, I had a letter from her saying, "I was right there with you in seat 1B, cheering you on." My favorite seat is 1A.

Often, I would drop in to her lovely colonial-style home in Oklahoma and play the piano for her. We would exchange ideas, laugh over mistakes and cheer each other's triumphs.

Even though she had sold her business at age 80 and "retired," she was still active. She spoke for me at large conventions and encouraged young people to grow and make a difference. She believed anyone could do anything they set their mind to do.

She told me that when she finally went to Heaven, she wanted me to sing a song for her family called "What a Wonderful World." She said, "I want them to remember me as one who loved life and believed in the possibilities all around us." With all of her family gathered around after her memorial service, we shared this song and the celebration of her life together.

This incredible woman taught me how to believe in myself and that one person can make a difference. As I studied Dr. Jenson's principles, I realized he was carrying on with Aunt Ethel's challenge - to build character and balance. It was the same lesson.

I encourage you to read *Achieving Authentic Success*. Adopt the MAXIMIZERS principles in the book and begin to make an impact on your world.

Be further challenged to keep these seven areas of your life in balance:

➤ Faith
➤ Fitness
➤ Family
➤ Friendship
➤ Finance
➤ Firm (Career)
➤ Fun.

As we work on keeping our lives balanced, we can focus more clearly without obstacles to our goals. It is extremely difficult to accomplish anything of significance if you do not have a plan, especially a written one. Take time each day, each month, each quarter, and certainly each year to evaluate what you have accomplished. Then, regroup and start again.

I found it vital to give myself small rewards commensurate with the task accomplished. This helped me to move forward. I believe vision is enhanced through times of rest – physical and emotional.

Letting ourselves have time off will help us recoup our energy and get the creative juices flowing again. During times of rest and relaxation, I find the vision grows. I am able to step back from the everyday work and see where I am headed and be refreshed.

A young organist in Russia taught me a great lesson on vision. His name? Boris Kleiner. He was from Minsk, Russia. My conductor friend, Helmuth Rilling, discovered him at a Bach Festival in Moscow when he was only 19. Professor Rilling is a leading expert on Bach today and travels in many countries teaching young people about this phenomenal man and his music. He called me and asked me if I would give Boris a scholarship to come to the United States for further musical study. I readily agreed.

The next summer, I met him in Oregon at the Bach Festival. I invited him to my home in Seattle, which housed a pipe organ with over forty ranks. There are about 100 pipes per rank, which means there are about 4,000 pipes. After making some adjustments to the organ, this amazing young man sat down and played Bach for two hours without music.

I asked him how he could have learned to play the organ so well in Russia, when all the churches were closed during the era of Communism. He told me he had built an organ of cardboard. He set up a small table and drew to scale four keyboards and stacked them on bricks. On the floor he had a cardboard pedal board, built to scale. For eight hours a day, he practiced on this paper instrument.

I asked him how that was possible.

"Oh, I could hear it in my mind," he answered.

This is visualization at its finest.

For only a half-hour each week, he was allowed to play the organ in the only cathedral in Moscow that remained open for the tourists. Until the following week, when he could play again, he kept those sounds in his mind. It worked. Boris now has a doctoral degree in music and performs all over Europe.

That's how you hold on to your dreams. It takes heart, belief, tenacity, and good old-fashioned hard work.

People often ask me what I did before I went into business for myself. "I created music with young people," I will say. Their eyes get soft and they say wistfully, "I remember being in a school musical when I was young. It was one of the greatest experiences of my life."

As a teacher, it's your job to believe that a young person can be transformed into a star. It is an amazing process to watch. Because of your belief, a star is born.

Whether it is business, music, sports, or an educational endeavor you desire, if you visualize the end result, you will achieve it. William James said: "That which holds our attention, determines our action."

Ask yourself two questions:

> ➤ What do I really want?

> ➤ Am I willing to ask for help?

Then, follow two simple rules:

- Set up a strategy to achieve it

- Make a commitment to someone who will hold you accountable

Remember, if it is to be, it's up to me!

6

The Life Changing Impact of Mentors—

Powerful Influences in Positive Thinking

By Ron Jenson

When I was a little kid, I was a hood, a hoodlum, a troublemaker. I was a little fat boy. They called me "Jelly Belly Jenson." I had freckles; they called me "Frecks." I had glasses, they called me "Specks."

I had a red nose from sunburn; they called me "Rudolph." I got in trouble at school. I had very, very poor grades. In fact, a couple of years ago my brother brought me my 4th grade report card from Mr. Kono. I had a D average. But for effort I received solid E's for Excellence.

Now, think of what that says to a little kid. "Ronnie, you are really stupid. But, you are maximizing your potential." That is how I saw my life. I was a big time loser who was doing all he could do.

Beyond all of this, I got in trouble with the law because I began hanging around with some young men who stole, forged checks and did other things they shouldn't do.

A mentor enters my life

And then at the low point, when I was a young teenager, something very dramatic happened. I had an experience at a conference that not only touched me at a deep spiritual level, but allowed me to meet an individual who began to pour his life into me. He became a short-term mentor/coach. Every time we met over a three- month period after the conference he would strain to find something to encourage. He worked hard at becoming a "raving fan" of mine.

One week he would say, "Ronnie, you talk a lot. Now, what you have to say isn't very constructive but you have some verbal skills and maybe one day you'll become a great speaker." The next week he would say, "Ronnie, kids follow you. Now, you aren't going the right direction but you have some leadership skills and one day you may become a great leader."

Every time we were together he *profoundly marked my life*. He said things like, "Ron, your life is significant. Ron, you're going to make a difference. Ron, you're going to help change the world. Ron, your life will be remembered as something that helped mark the history of mankind."

You know, the more he said these things to me, a real failure in most areas of my life, the more I started to believe him. So much so that in several months my grades went from D's to A's and stayed there the rest of my life. I went from being well overweight to losing weight and becoming a high achieving athlete in a number of fields. I went from getting into constant fights at school to becoming popular at the school, well liked, and the student body President.

Think about it: I went from doing the wrong things to doing the right things. I went from not liking people to really honestly caring for people. I went from not achieving to beginning to achieve in all major areas of my life. Do you know why? It's because someone believed in me.

He mentored me! I can't remember that much of what he taught me, but his life marked me forever. It didn't take years or even many months but 10-12 weeks of meeting together. That did the trick. It began a life change because someone came along side me and gave himself to me.

That's what can happen in your life and through you in the lives of others as you learn to mentor, encourage and express confidence.

Leaving a lasting legacy

And you know what? A significant part of the legacy you lead is the people you have touched—those you have marked profoundly.

I'll never forget interviewing a close friend of mine, Bob Safford, a world class leader with a wonderful family, extraordinary set of friends and business associates, a fabulous life style and an organization that few have ever dreamed possible. I asked Bob this question—"At the end of your life how will you know you've succeeded?"

His response was classic. "Ron, I guess I would know by the number of people who wept at my funeral."

Do you get his point? He was interested in leaving a legacy of changed lives—people who would profoundly miss him because of his lasting impact on them. He is well down the road in leaving just that kind of legacy.

What about YOU?

What kind of impact are you having on the people around you as a mentor and a coach? And, are you satisfied with the results—not just from a cash flow and/or business perspective, but also from a personal, significant impact perspective. Are you seeing lives changed?

Someone who is succeeding in all of life authentically cares for people. That's his *modus operandi.* That's his normal method of living. That's his absolute. I might have to discipline someone. I might have to bring about some change in someone's life, but my motivation is always the same- to really care about people. To authentically love people. And one of the best ways to do that is to express confidence in people.

Warren James said it this way, "The deepest longing in the human heart is that longing to be appreciated." I have seen that to be true of people in all walks of life. The poor have the need; the rich have the need. Those who are not known have the need; the famous have the need. All people have a tremendous need to be appreciated. They need to have someone express confidence in them. As that confidence is expressed, they begin to believe in themselves and experience their own confidence. Then they are able, through proper motivation, to begin doing the right kinds of things and becoming truly successful.

Do you believe in people?

What do you do when someone fails you? My tendency is to rub their face in it. Instead, the appropriate thing is to express confidence in that person.

Do you know how fleas are trained? This is a silly story, but it works. They put them in a little jar, and these little fleas keep jumping up and hitting their heads on the lid of the jar. After a while these fleas say, "I'm getting tired of hitting my head on the top of the jar. If I jump up a shorter distance, I won't hit my head." So they jump up a shorter distance. Then the top is removed from the jar. The fleas could jump out but they don't because they've been trained to jump only so high.

I want to suggest to you that many of us have been trained to jump only so high in life. We've been told our whole lives, whether by the state or by our family or by own internal fears, "You can only do so much. You can only jump this high. This is all you can do. You're not that significant. You're not that important. You're not a person of worth. You're really only an average kind of individual. You really can't make a difference." And we only jump so high.

How about you?

Are you soaring and maximizing your potential? Or, have you given in to the conditioning of your background and negative comments from others?

This is why positive impact from others becomes so important.

I saw how my life was changed because of someone believing in me. And I can look back at hundreds of lives during my lifetime, people who've been touched simply because at times when I've thought of it and when I've been consistent to this principle, I've said, "I believe in you."

A great speaker I admire tells a story of when he was a young boy in the fifth grade He was such a bad little boy his teacher had to tie him to his chair. On the day he entered sixth grade, his new teacher knelt down in front of him and said,

"So you're Howie Hendricks? I've heard a lot about you." He thought, "Uh-oh, I'm dead."

Then she looked him right in the eyes and said, "And you know what? I don't believe a word of it."

She expressed confidence.

Do you know what happened to Howie Hendricks? He was dramatically changed because someone believed in him.

May I suggest to you today that you need to find someone toward whom you can express confidence? Find someone at work or in your home. Both articulate verbally or in writing appreciation for some specific area of their life and watch the results.

Sister Helen P. Mrosla tells the following story that drives home this concept of the power of a mentor who encourages those around him or her.

He was in the first third grade class I taught at Saint Mary's School in Morris, Minnesota. All 34 of my students were dear to me, but Mark Eklund was one in a million. Very neat in appearance, but had that happy-to-be-alive attitude that made even his occasional mischievousness delightful. Mark talked incessantly. I had to remind him again and again that talking without permission was not acceptable.

What impressed me so much, though, was his sincere response every time I had to correct him for misbehaving. "Thank you for correcting me, Sister!" I didn't know what to make of it at first, but before long I became accustomed to hearing it many times a day.

One morning my patience was growing thin when Mark talked once too often, and then I made a novice teacher's mistake. I looked at Mark and said, "If you say one more word, I am going to tape your mouth shut!"

It wasn't ten seconds later when Chuck blurted out, "Mark is talking again." I hadn't asked any of the students to help me watch Mark, but since I had stated the punishment in front of the class, I had to act on it. I remember the scene as if it had occurred this morning. I walked to my desk, very deliberately opened my drawer and took out a roll of masking tape.

Without saying a word, I proceeded to Mark's desk, tore off two pieces of tape and made a big X with them over his mouth. I then returned to the front of the room. As I glanced at Mark to see how he was doing, he winked at me. That did it!! I started laughing. The class cheered as I walked back to Mark's desk, removed the tape, and shrugged my shoulders.

His first words were, "Thank you for correcting me, Sister."

At the end of the year, I was asked to teach junior high math. The years flew by, and before I knew it Mark was in my classroom again. He was more handsome than ever and just as polite.

Since he had to listen carefully to my instruction in the "new math," he did not talk as much in ninth grade as he had in third. One Friday, things just didn't feel right. We had worked hard on a new concept all week, and I sensed that the students were frowning, frustrated with themselves and edgy with one another. I had to stop this crankiness before it got out of hand. So I asked them to list the names of the other students in the room on two sheets of paper, leaving a space between each name. Then I told them to think of the nicest thing they could say about each of their classmates and write it down.

It took the remainder of the class period to finish their assignment, and as the students left the room, each one handed me the papers. Charlie smiled. Mark said, "Thank you for teaching me, Sister. Have a good weekend."

That Saturday, I wrote down the name of each student on a separate sheet of paper, and I listed what everyone else had said about that individual.

On Monday I gave each student his or her list. Before long, the entire class was smiling. "Really?" I heard whispered. "I never knew that meant anything to anyone!" "I didn't know others liked me so much." No one ever mentioned those papers in class again. I never knew if they discussed them after class or with their parents, but it didn't matter. The exercise had accomplished its purpose. The students were happy with themselves and one another again. That group of students moved on.

Several years later, after I returned from vacation, my parents met me at the airport. As we were driving home, Mother asked me the usual questions about the trip—the weather, my experiences in general. There was a lull in the conversation.

Mother gave Dad a sideways glance and simply says, "Dad?" My father cleared his throat as he usually did before something important. "The Eklunds called last night," he began.

"Really?" I said. "I haven't heard from them in years. I wonder how Mark is." Dad responded quietly. "Mark was killed in Vietnam," he said. "The funeral is tomorrow, and his parents would like it if you could attend."

To this day I can still point to the exact spot on I-494 where Dad told me about Mark. I had never seen a serviceman in a military coffin before. Mark looked so handsome, so mature. All I could think at that moment was, "Mark I would give all the masking tape in the world if only you would talk to me."

The church was packed with Mark's friends. Chuck's sister sang "The Battle Hymn of the Republic." Why did it have to rain on the day of the funeral? It was difficult enough at the graveside. The pastor said the usual prayers, and the bugler played taps. One by one those who loved Mark took a last walk by the coffin and sprinkled it with holy water. I was the last one to bless the coffin.

As I stood there, one of the soldiers who acted as pallbearer came up to me. "Were you Mark's math teacher?" he asked. I nodded as I continued to stare at the coffin. "Mark talked about you a lot," he said.

After the funeral, most of Mark's former classmates headed to Chuck's farmhouse for lunch. Mark's mother and father were there, obviously waiting for me.

"We want to show you something," his father said, taking a wallet out of his pocket. They found this on Mark when he was killed. We thought you might recognize it.

Opening the billfold, he carefully removed two worn pieces of notebook paper that had obviously been taped, folded and refolded many times. I knew without looking that the papers were the ones on which I had listed all the good things each of Mark's classmates had said about him.

"Thank you so much for doing that," Mark's mother said. "As you can see, Mark treasured it." Mark's classmates started to gather around us. Charlie smiled rather sheepishly and said, "I still have my list. It's in the top drawer of my desk at home."

Chuck's wife said, "Chuck asked me to put his in our wedding album." I have mine too," Marilyn said. "It's in my diary." Then Vicki, another classmate, reached into her pocketbook, took out her wallet and showed her worn and frazzled list to the group. "I carry this with me at all times," Vicki said without batting an eyelash.

"I think we all saved our lists." That's when I finally sat down and cried.

I cried for Mark and for all his friends who would never see him again.

The density of people in society is so thick that we forget that life will end one day. And we don't know when that one-day will be. So please, tell the people you love and care for, that they are special and important. Tell them, before it is too late.

So, what about *you*?

Can you take the step of being a mentor—pouring your life into other people? This chapter should drive home the point that your steps don't need to be big ones just little steps— encouraging people with a note, a word, or focused attention and become a raving fan of those people around you.

Start with your family and then those in your business and friendship community. Find something they are doing well and articulate it in print or verbal. Express confidence and compliment these people.

Be concrete (specific). Focus on character and skills that you see. Do it consistently. Make it a habit to coach and mentor those around you with words of encouragement and watch their worlds change.

Hey, watch your *own* world change! Get excited and enthused, you are on the road to building and maintaining an always positive attitude in your business!

7

Self-Discipline Creates An Always Positive Attitud

By Jack Daughery

As a young boy, I learned the importance of self-discipline long before I understood the true power it can bring. While other boys my age spent afternoons playing baseball or fishing, I was hard at work in the fields. Our family worked as migrants, traveling from farm to farm, pruning grapevines, picking fruit or harvesting the seasonal crops. It was hard life, from which I learned many valuable lessons.

Over the years, I have learned a great deal about success and power of the mind. Some of my lessons were learned from the School of Hard Knocks, while others came from careful study of the philosophy of success. I have had the high honor and privilege of mentoring many great and successful men with whom I have shared my lessons and perspective from life. Of all the lessons I have learned, the most important is that *Self-discipline Creates an Always Positive Attitude.*

What is selfdiscipline?

Self-administered discipline is the highest form of discipline. Many people from different perspectives have defined self-discipline. I define self-discipline as the act of controlling one's mind to overcome the obstacles that can prevent the achievement of desired results. It simply means the ability to take complete possession of your own mind.

Once one has attained this high degree of mental power, virtually anything is possible. A person who has the ability to attain desired results in almost any circumstance will always enjoy a positive mental attitude and will attract others who will assist in the attainment of the desired objective.

Self discipline is a choice governed by habit

The decision to become self-disciplined is a choice. Once the choice evolves to a decision, it must be consistently subjected to a daily routine that reinforces it. Then, the decision no longer seems a choice at all. Battles of self-discipline are waged and lost daily by the untrained mind. One need only look at the physical and financial picture of America today to see such evidence. There are more overweight, broke people than ever before. Masters of self-discipline are able to control every aspect of their lives by making decisions and reinforcing them until they become habits.

Virtually every action in your life has been reinforced with repetition. From the very first steps as a child to the pace of a marathoner, repetition plays a key role in performance. To successfully acquire self-discipline you must be able to:

(1) Transform your desires into a clear objective

(2) Consistently reinforce and repeat your decision each day with action and thought habits

(3) Immediately act when the opportunity to advance your objective presents itself daily

This is the most effective process for acquiring any habit - good or bad.

Regardless of the decision to pursue a good habit or a bad habit, once the habit is cast, the person becomes the servant of that choice. The choice will govern that aspect of their life automatically. People who lack self-discipline often choose the easy path, even when it is not the right path. Then, they become the servants of that wrong choice.

Many refuse to choose for fear of making a wrong choice. That also becomes a decision. Masters of self-discipline make choices based on accurate thought and diligently pursue a course of action that reinforces the decision until it becomes a habit. When one has mastered self-discipline, small tasks or great projects may be accomplished with ease and speed.

Lessons from life

Over the years, I have learned many lessons from life. Lessons from my youth and experiences later in life demonstrate the value of self-discipline and how it creates a positive mental attitude.

My father set high expectations for my younger brother and me. Our responsibilities were not to be taken lightly. As young boys, we worked during the winter pruning grapevines. It was cold and our hands would numb in the frigid air. At the end of the row, my father had placed a small bucket of burning stove oil. The fire warmed our hands and provided respite when we were tired and cold.

While my brother and I would have preferred to work near the fire all day, my father insisted we prune two rows before we warmed our hands. When we were finally able to warm our hands, the warmth of the fire seemed that much warmer and we felt better for having "toughed it out." At an early age, I witnessed the power of the mind to overcome circumstance.

Whenever we were in a place long enough, we planted a garden. It was a vital source of food for our family. One of our chores was to weed the garden. We would give it a lick and a promise while our minds planned our next adventure. After a brief effort, we went off to play.

Of course, my father would inspect our job and if not done right, we would have to do it again. Soon, it became a challenge to make sure the job was done right before he inspected. We would perform more than we thought he would expect so that we could play without having to do the job again. It felt great when he was pleased with our efforts. I didn't understand it then, but I was being taught the art of going the extra mile.

The future is in your control

I learned these simple lessons and many more from the hard life of my youth. As I grew older, I learned the lessons were more important because the decisions I made in life became more critical. When I was old enough, my dad got me a job at a local potato plant where he worked. It was hard, punishing labor. During harvest season I would work 18 hours a day. I often slept in a small bed at the plant. I was married to the job. I treated the job as if it were *my* business.

I climbed the ladder until I was the Warehouse Manager. My goal was to be General Manager but the position was given to an owner's son-in-law. No matter how hard I worked, I was not able to move further up the ladder. I was a young ambitious man with nowhere left to go.

When I realized I was not going to rise to the top, I began to get frustrated. I wanted more and worked harder than anyone I knew. I was quickly becoming disillusioned with the concept of becoming successful. It seemed like my success was in the hands of someone other than myself.

Soon thereafter, we were presented with an extraordinary business concept. I was offered the chance to start my own business. Everything was my own responsibility, and I had to subsidize my entire involvement in the operation.

At a time when money was tight, it was not an easy choice. Yet, when I understood I could determine *my* destiny by *my* performance, it became a challenge I had to accept.

I continued to work at the warehouse while I pursued my business. After eighteen months of effort, we had begun to see some glimmer of success. The business had not yet produced enough results to warrant leaving my job. Yet, the harvest season was approaching and I would soon be enduring grueling eighteen-hour days. I knew if I took time off from our business to work my job, our business would suffer. We were at a major "fork in the road."

This was not an easy decision. We had little money in the bank, children to feed and bills to pay. Yet, I knew if we were ever to achieve financial independence, it was now or never. After some deliberate thought and careful planning, we chose the path less traveled. We chose freedom. We would soon learn the decision came with a cost.

The responsibility for success is yours

We live in a society that encourages people to blame their failures on others. Self-disciplined people refuse to make excuses and accept responsibility for their actions. The majority of people let others influence their choices or accept whatever comes their way as inevitable. You must openly express your positive objectives to yourself and resolve to achieve them every day. Most people realize which issues in life are most troubling to them. But instead of resolving those issues, they act confused as the pressure mounts.

Effective self-suggestion requires your focus be on achieving a positive outcome to your issues. This, too, is a habit of self-discipline. Your thoughts are *your* responsibility.

Striking out on my own required a new mindset – a mindset with which I was unfamiliar. To be successful, I had to study others who had already succeeded. I spent hundreds of hours reading books and studying the philosophy of success. Taking responsibility for my own actions without a boss telling me what to do next was a critical step in my growth as a self-disciplined person. Reading is the surest way to improve your chance for success. I read my way out of poverty.

Make daily progress toward your goal

I had many new challenges and obstacles to overcome. I set out with determination and absolute conviction I would succeed. I had to succeed. My family was counting on me, and my "friends" were all watching to see if I would be successful. I immediately set in place a daily routine and focused my efforts on actions to improve my business.

Seemingly meaningless steps were key to my success - smiling at the grocery clerk, saying hello to strangers. These small gestures helped me overcome my shyness. I once rode an elevator all day just so I could learn to get over my fear of talking to people. I was developing the habit of making daily progress.

We had a lot of work ahead of us. It's a good thing we can only see a little ways ahead. If I had seen how much mental and physical work was involved, I may have been overwhelmed. I chipped away at the issues that held me back by making progress each day.

Leaders become effective with practice. To be most effective, you must perform every day. Perform, despite the fears or challenges and make daily progress toward your goal. All successful people experience many challenges and tests. Keep your thoughts focused on the vision of the finish line by making daily progress toward your goal, and you will find success with time and consistent effort.

Focus on the desired goal for success

Your thoughts are critical – keep them focused on the desired goal of success. Regardless of what goal you direct your thoughts, good or bad, it will come to fruition. The masses feed their mind on what they don't want. This is because they have not disciplined their minds to banish fear. Despite efforts to the contrary, the average person gets exactly what he or she doesn't want because so many thoughts have been directed toward the worst possible outcome.

Your thought habits are food for your mind to consume. In the beginning, you may make some poor decisions about your goals. For example, I started smoking as a teenager because I wanted to be like my buddies who smoked.

The first time I tried, I turned green, coughed, and felt like throwing up. I ignored the obvious evidence that suggested smoking was a very bad idea. But, I was determined to smoke like my buddies, so I made myself do it for several months.

Finally, after awhile, with consistent repetition and discipline, I developed the smoking habit.

Years later, I would pay the price for focusing on the wrong goal. Instead of focusing on what my "buddies" thought, I should have focused on my personal health. Fortunately, it was not too late to reverse a habit and I made the decision to quit.

Fixing bad habits can be very difficult. My body had become addicted, so I had to start all over and develop the discipline to be a non-smoker. Several weeks later, the physical part was done but the psychological aspect of took much longer. Finally after a period of time, the thoughts weren't there any more.

It's important to inspect all your habits to see which need weeded out, and which you need to keep. Focus on your desired goal and you can avoid adopting habits that are not productive. If you'll apply these same principles to anything you desire in life, you can achieve them. *It is an exciting and happier way of life.*

Your mindset determines...*Your success!*

As we have developed our business, we have faced many challenges. By far, the key to surviving challenges is found by applying the proper mindset. Early on, the group responsible for assisting us in the development of our business quit. They had gotten disenchanted with their business, and didn't want to keep putting in the effort anymore. We weighed the facts, considered our circumstances, and decided it was our goal to build our business and be free. I searched until I found someone who was successful and willing to assist with our objectives

We cast our dreams in stone and set our mindset to succeed. We had already burned too many bridges to go back, and *quit,* wasn't part of our make-up. Your mindset will allow you to overcome potentially negative circumstances and ultimately determines your success.

Commit to the race

Self-disciplined people have the ability to remain committed to the race even when it seems difficult. In an effort to show how healthy we were, my wife (Rita) and I committed to running a marathon. We researched and talked to people who had completed the race. We committed to the marathon, and began a training program three or four months out from the race date.

A week or two into the training, my mind started coming up with excuses:

- I didn't like doing this
- It wasn't necessary
- I seemingly had better things to do with my time

I found myself in a battle – with myself. If not for the power of self-discipline and the accountability to my wife, I may have submitted to my negative self.

After two months of solid training, I experienced a major setback. I pulled a hamstring and was in real pain. Many things crossed my mind. I knew if I didn't do this race now, I never would. I knew my wife would run by herself, and not do another marathon with me. I had invested too much mental and physical effort to do anything but commit to the race.

I had no options. I had to put my mind to work on how to make it happen. I made daily trips to a physical therapist and cut down my running times. Slowly and surely, because I was committed to the race, *I was able to improve my physical condition.*

We weren't out to set any speed records. We just wanted to finish the course of 26.2 miles.

Race day was perfect. The excitement of the other runners fueled our adrenaline, while the cool, crisp air made us feel very alive. We were prepared. Now would come the test.

The first ten miles were very easy. The next five weren't so bad. At the 15-mile mark, it got tougher. By the 20-mile mark, the effort took real willpower. I relied on our earlier commitment to the race and the self-discipline acquired during training.

I will never forget the victory of finishing and the emotional high I felt in reaching for the victory T-shirt. Moments later, Rita and I embraced after she crossed the line with the same feeling of excitement and accomplishment.

Life is a series of choices. In most cases, circumstances don't determine your lifestyle. What determines your lifestyle is what you do with your circumstances. When you are truly committed to the race, you will overcome setbacks and achieve your goals despite physical or mental challenges.

Stretch for goals higher than yourself

It is critical to set your goals high. Most people will set goals at a level they know they can easily achieve. Every new goal is an opportunity to stretch the boundaries of yourself and achieve something greater than you expected. Consistently stretching for goals forces you to go the "extra mile."

The success will not always be found in the last mile. Often, it is only found in the "extra mile." When you wait until it's comfortable to reach a goal, it never gets done. Then, the tendency becomes easier and easier to "put off until tomorrow what should be done today."

Several times during the course of our business, we have been faced with a goal that seemed unreachable. With the help and inspiration of others, we have stretched ourselves to reach a goal. One goal I remember required the assistance of many people to accomplish. This was a goal that proved we could not only lead our own business, but we could teach leadership skills to six others who would also enjoy success. This goal was considered a pinnacle accomplishment in the industry.

For several years we were unable to accomplish our goal. We experienced many setbacks, and paid a big price to finally achieve the goal. When were finished, we had not only achieved success but also helped six other businesses achieve success. What a feeling to know we had helped others achieve their goals. Despite many setbacks and we finally achieved success.

We achieve success because we have set a goal higher than our comfort level. We were committed and other people were counting on us to succeed. This compelled us to work harder and sacrifice more. When our goal was finally accomplished, the return was far greater than we had imagined.

Accurate thought is the sign of a self-disciplined mind

Accurate thought is the act of separating opinions and emotion from fact. Over time, a self-disciplined mind becomes capable of accurate thought at ALL times. The ability to think accurately will assure your efforts are focused on the right goals and not burdened with distractions. Everyone needs a mentor who is an accurate thinker. This person should be an example of self-discipline and control.

At times, when physically tired, I find the need to closely monitor my thoughts, as my mind becomes unguarded. Don't let emotions and imagination get out of the supervision of the your reason. They can be a potentially damaging combination if left unchecked. Strict discipline on your thought patterns will ensure your thoughts are accurate and as productive as possible.

Action plan for success

An action plan to become a master of self-discipline must first begin with a decision. If you want to become self-disciplined, you must first commit to reinforce your decision every day. Any resolution or decision you make today has to be made again tomorrow. Not only that, but it has to be kept each day. If you miss one day in keeping it, you have to go back and begin all over again.

Self-discipline is an acquired trait of character. You can't grab it from somebody else and take it on. You can't buy it. It doesn't sneak up and grab you. You must develop it from within. When you have accomplished this, you will have a life full of peace and harmony. It will astound you as you look around at the chaos in which people live their lives. You will discover that you will rise above. You'll find it's a way of living that is just short of miraculous.

Daily habits

Over time, I developed a series of daily activities that have formed the foundation of my self-disciplined nature. Initially, it took conscious action to complete these tasks. Over time, they became habit and took on power. These activities are part of my daily *habit force* and are so ingrained in my life were I not to perform one, I would feel as though I cheated my way through the day.

Daily habit forces of a self-disciplined mind

1. **Read Every Day** - Spend at least 15 minutes per day reading a book that positively influences your character. These may be inspirational, motivational, or self-improvement in nature. Biographies of successful leaders are encouraged as additional reading.

2. **Spend Time in Daily Preparation** – Prepare for every day by planning your daily activities. Write down each daily objective and when complete, cross it off the list. The objective you list as #1 everyday should be your Definite Major Purpose.

3. **Exercise Daily** – The importance of physical fitness cannot be over emphasized. Proper physical fitness is essential to maintaining a self-disciplined mind and the most apparent trait of a self-disciplined individual. You should spend 20 to 40 minutes daily in some form of physical activity.

4. **Perform Every Day** – Each day perform some objective that will move you closer to your Definite Major Purpose. Rarely will a day pass when you cannot accomplish something to advance you toward your ultimate purpose.

5. **Use Self-Suggestion to Reinforce your Goals** – Self-suggestion is the first and most important aspect of self-discipline. Define each objective as a desirable goal and establish thought and physical patterns that result in habits conducive to your goals.

The promise of self discipline

Here's the promise of developing the habit of self-discipline. If you develop the habit of making your promise each morning and keeping it each day, you will finally wake up one morning a different person in a different world. You will wonder what has happened to the world you used to live in. Your positive attitude will be a direct reflection of the inner strength and character you have developed with self-discipline. The promise is self-discipline creates an *always positive attitude*.

That promise requires you to examine each area of your life, and with accurate thought, decide which areas need improvement or change. If change is needed, you must set up an action plan and pursue it diligently. Each personality must examine his or her situation differently. We each have strengths and weaknesses, and you must understand what yours are. Your mentor can assist you with this process.

Before we understood, my wife and I used to waste lots of time "butting heads" over different ways we looked at things. Today, we sometimes laugh at our different personalities. We have learned to leverage our individual strengths to achieve great power. By focusing on our strengths, we overcame individual weakness and achieved harmony.

Today, we enjoy phenomenal success in everything we do. When you are willing to surrender to your purpose, then the desires of your heart are only a matter of time and concerted and self-disciplined effort.

A gift to be developed and used wisely

After years of observation, I can quickly determine if an individual has a self-disciplined nature. I need only observe a few traits of the person before I can determine if they are self-disciplined. It is a developed trait that is quite easy to spot.

If you are prepared to enjoy the life as a self-disciplined person, I encourage you to spend time with others who have developed the trait. Through study and talking to your mentor (carefully chosen) ask them questions about discipline and encourage honest appraisal. Be willing to listen and learn and not take it as criticism. There is an old saying, "When the student is ready, the teacher will appear."

When you have been given a gift that transforms your whole life, it's like being Cinderella. The person is transformed from a life of drudgery and non-importance to a life of wonder, significance and abundance. I believe this is how we are meant to live.

Who could have predicted the son of migrant workers could become a leader and mentor to many?

Wow!

What a wonderful world!

8

Get Out of the Vacuum – Go Build

By Jim Floor

"The average person puts only 25 percent of his energy and ability into his work. The world takes off its hat to those who put more than 50 percent of their capacity, and stands on its head for those few and far between souls who devote 100 percent."

- Andrew Carnegie

We've all heard about three kinds of people in the world – those who make things happen, those who watch things happen, and those who wonder what happened. The truth is, all of us have found ourselves bouncing in and out of each of these categories, depending on our personal circumstances. The key to ultimately becoming someone who consistently MAKES THINGS HAPPEN in a positive and productive way is developing the proper attitude and habits.

For most of us, that requires change, which is often uncomfortable and even painful. And yet, most people are closer to achieving their dreams and goals than they realize. In fact, we are typically just one quality decision away. It is a decision to get started and not quit until the job is finished.

Our story

When Margee and I got started in our own business, I was employed by a large Los Angeles-based corporation. My responsibility was to establish and maintain a working relationship with the Los Angeles City Council and the Mayor's Office, which required several evening commitments each month.

Therefore, to build our business, we had to learn to prioritize our time, schedule appointments or meetings two or three nights per week, and consistently and persistently work toward our dreams and goals.

After 15 months of doing just that, and experiencing both personal and business growth, I was offered a significant promotion within the corporation. This promotion would require moving our family 400 miles north to Sacramento, the state capital of California. I would be responsible for making contacts in the Governor's Office and State Legislature, which I knew, would require a steep learning curve and major time commitment. However, I was confident that once I got settled, I would quickly return to building our business as we had before.

But during the next three months, I flew from Los Angeles to Sacramento each Monday morning, returning to Los Angeles on Thursday evenings. I quickly got out of the habit of doing the things necessary to continue building our business. Of course, I promised myself I would get started just as soon as we moved our family to Sacramento, enrolled the kids into new schools and got back into a routine. But once we did, I found every excuse imaginable to continue to procrastinate - buying and furnishing a new home, finding the right church, getting through the legislative session, and building a new list of contacts.

They were convenient excuses for putting off the decision to get started until tomorrow. Another excuse - there was no support system in the greater Sacramento area. Fortunately, we continued to listen to tapes and read books. We also took the three-hour drive (one way) to attend the only business seminars being conducted in Northern California each month. Those seminars only served as a painful reminder to me that I wasn't doing what I had committed to do.

Another six months passed before I became angry enough with myself to make a quality decision to move on. Thankfully we had stayed plugged into the system during the transition, but we went to work with a greater sense of purpose - a desire to create enough income to enable me to leave my corporate career without concern for our financial security.

During the next 20 months, we sold out totally to building our business without compromising our higher priorities of God, family, country and job. We suddenly found ourselves free to pursue our business and our dreams on a full-time basis.

What made the difference? Two things:

1. I stopped making excuses and rationalizations.

2. I got started immediately and didn't stop until I was free.

When some people learned I had left a promising sixteen-year career with a major corporation at the age of forty-one, they believed we must have been really lucky. I suppose in some ways we were lucky – we didn't give up on our dreams or ourselves.

Luck and diligent work

You could say that luck is a major player in the game of life. Thomas Jefferson said, "I am a great believer in luck, and I find the harder I work the more I have of it." King Solomon, the author of many proverbs, preceded him with these words; "Lazy people want much but get little, while the diligent are prospering." Do we succeed by luck? Only when that luck is created by lots of hard work.

Most of us would like to succeed. Most of us somehow feel a sense of entitlement to success. You have seen that success is not just a matter of money, fame or power. Success comes through the diligence of becoming all that God wants us to be.

During that process, we sometimes stumble over the crutch of laziness. How do you keep from failing to measure up to what you "coulda, woulda, shoulda" been?

How do you find internal motivation to keep up the fight? How do you tackle life rather than allowing life to run over you? You throw away the crutch called laziness.

You can get a new grip on life when you realize the importance of three integral elements, which you must master:

- The lasting defeat of the problem of procrastination as a habit and hindrance.

- Learning the life process of evaluating and eliminating the useless and damaging from your life.
- Making discipline an essential and effective part of your character.

If you have ever struggled with the dreaded adversary called procrastination, you can rest assured that you have had some famous company. Throughout history, people have struggled with how to motivate themselves to action.

It is said that the French novelist Victor Hugo ordered his servants to confiscate his clothes and not return them until his scheduled writing time was completed. Demosthenes, a Greek philosopher, reportedly shaved one side of his head so that he would be ashamed to be seen in Public.

I've even heard of a chartered Procrastinator's Club whose members live by the credo, "If you put off enough things until later, you'll discover that most of them didn't need to be done in the first place." This, from a group famous for its fun and festive annual Christmas party - held religiously each June.

If you are like most, you sometimes suffer from the desire to put off until tomorrow what could be done today. In fact, Dr. William Knaus, in *U.S. News & World Report*, writes that as many as ninety percent of us suffer from procrastination.

It is certainly not unnatural to procrastinate concerning taking out the trash and cleaning the house. But Dr. Knaus suggests that, while it is common and harmless to procrastinate on those unpleasant tasks you don't enjoy, your procrastination tends to become a natural part of your regular behavior.

Problems occur when your procrastination becomes a lifestyle pattern, which leads to mediocrity in numerous areas of your life. Can you live with procrastination that costs you significant amounts of time, money, personal fulfillment, and success?

To procrastinate in ways that cause us to fail to reach our goals or fail to realize our potential should certainly be unacceptable to us all. The truth is that there is a heavy price that comes with the habit of procrastination. Nothing can be sadder than looking back on life and saying, "If only ... I wish I had ... Why did I wait so long to ... I can't believe I didn't..."

We love John Greenleaf Whittier's statement, "For of all sad words of tongue or pen, the saddest are these: "It might have been!" Perhaps the heaviest price of procrastination comes in the form of lost opportunities to better their lives, save their families, turn to God, or improve their financial situations. While you are busy postponing, life is busy passing you by. Sometimes, opportunity doesn't knock twice. You have to be ready to jump when opportunity calls.

King Solomon, the author of many proverbs and to many, the wisest man who ever lived, put it bluntly when he said, "A lazy fellow has trouble all through life." Procrastination has an incredible way of turning a simple problem into a crisis and a routine situation into a disaster.

Procrastination multiples our problems. George H. Lorimer once said, "Putting off an easy thing makes it hard, and putting off a hard one makes it impossible." Who knows how many of our difficulties are of our own doing? Samuel Smiles has said, "It will generally be found that men who are constantly lamenting their ill luck are only reaping the consequences of their own neglect, mismanagement, and improvidence." In every area, procrastination multiplies our difficulties.

In fact, it was Benjamin Franklin who coined the phrase, "Never leave till tomorrow that which you can do today." The problem with procrastination is that it hurts lots of people, not simply those who clean up the messes. Sometimes you put things off out of fear...

✓ Fear of that career change

✓ Fear of that phone call

Sometimes you procrastinate as a way of exerting control over a situation or person. You may not be able to erase your bills, but you can put them off. You may not have the final say with your boss, but you can drag your feet. You can even procrastinate by busying yourself in all the wrong activities.

The world is full of busy-buts
(people busy ... but doing the wrong things).

It is, unfortunately, all too easy to find yourself in the unsavory position of the grasshopper in Aesop's fable, "the Grasshopper and the Ant."

> *Presently up came a grasshopper and begged the ants to spare her a few grains, "For," she said, "I am simply starving." The ants stopped work for a moment, though this was against their principles.*

> *"May we ask," said they, "what were you doing with yourself all last summer? Why didn't you collect a store of food for the winter?"*

> *"The fact is," replied the grasshopper, "I was so busy singing that I hadn't the time."*

The bottom line is...procrastinating hurts you personally

Procrastination keeps you from reaching your goals. It contributes to not feeling good about yourself. Even worse, it hurts your family, friends, and business associates. You may realize you are putting things off, and hope this will motivate you to stop procrastinating. Procrastination is such an ingrained behavior, making it a difficult cycle to break. So what is the answer?

The answer

It is amazing how we try to con ourselves and rationalize our own self-defeating behavior. Call it what you like – deferring, postponing, suspending, putting on the back burner, keeping in a holding pattern or calling a time-out. Procrastination is procrastination by any name, and it is likely that you don't need anyone else to prove that point to you.

What you want is someone to give you some practical steps to help you master the dreaded nemesis. The question remains, how do you prevail over procrastination? We live by the adage, "Anyone can show me my problem, but I'll love the one who shows me how to overcome it."

For many of us, procrastination is nothing more than a bad habit. A counterproductive mindset that can be the result of fear, frustration, past failures, perfectionism or any number of other unresolved personal issues. This is no way to live.

The key to conquering the habit of procrastination and postponing is this – developing the right attitude. Widely read author Chuck Swindoll sums up the importance of attitude about as well as we've seen it done. "The longer I live, the more I realize the impact of attitude on life." Chuck goes on to say, "Attitude, to me, is more important than facts. It is more important than the past, than education, than what other people think or say or do. It is more important than appearance, giftedness, or skill."

There is a great deal in life that is beyond our control. You cannot change the past. You have only a limited future. You have little or no say in the way some people will act. An infinite number of circumstances are outside of your power.

But one thing you can control is your attitude. No one can affect your attitude unless you give someone permission. Swindoll later says, "I am convinced that life is ten percent what happens to me and ninety percent how I react to it." Of the many things that attitude affects, procrastination is one of the most significant. Develop the right attitude and beat procrastination.

Someone once said that the opposite of procrastination is decision. In other words, to procrastinate is to postpone making a decision. If you think about when you procrastinate and what you procrastinate about, you will discover exactly how true that is. You put off paying bills because you never really decide when you are going to do it. You just leave it out there as something you need to do. You don't really want to do it, so it keeps getting pushed down the list. Soon they are past due. You don't clean the garage because it is just something that you need to do. You know it should be done, but it's not a job you want to start.

The result – it does not get done. There really is a simple way to solve this situation:

- Decide to do it
- Schedule it
- Do it on schedule

Forget about all these expressions: I need to...I plan to...I hope to...I can. Decide.

Margee always said that building the business was exhilarating, but just thinking about building it was exhausting. Procrastination is mentally exhausting. It is a heavy weight, which is bearing down on you constantly.

To make a decision and follow through with it is exhilarating. A quality decision is specific (date and time). A quality decision is concrete (it can hold up under accountability).

It is impossible for procrastination and decision to live in the same household. To understand that can be revolutionary and transformational. Soon your decisive attitude will reap benefits of more time for yourself, more accomplishments, a better feeling about yourself, and a break-up of the habit of procrastination.

Have you ever noticed how other people have excuses, and we have reasons? We almost always have good reasons why we have put something off. Benjamin Franklin said, "The people who are good at making excuses are rarely good at anything else." King Solomon said in Proverbs, "A lazy man is full of excuses. 'I can't go to work! If I go outside I might meet a lion in the street and be killed!'"

We can laugh at such an absurd excuse, but if we are honest with ourselves, we will realize our excuses are no better. I ran across these true statements (excuses) taken from submitted insurance forms:

- "Going home from work I drove into the wrong house and collided with a tree I don't have."

- "The guy was all over the road, I had to swerve a number of times to hit him…"

- "As I pulled away from the side of the road, I glanced at my mother-in-law and headed over the embankment."

- "In my attempt to kill a fly I ran into a telephone pole."

- "I was on my way to the doctor with rear end trouble when my universal joints gave way, causing me to have an accident."

- "I had been driving my car for forty years when I fell asleep at the wheel and had an accident."

- "The telephone pole was approaching fast. I attempted to swerve off its path when it struck my front end."

And my favorite:

- "The pedestrian had no idea which way to go, so I ran over him."

What's your excuse?

What is it in your life that you know you need to change, but you've been putting it off? What do you know you need to do, but you haven't done? To prevail over procrastination, you must decide that excuses are no longer a valid part of your way of thinking.

Changing your attitude is something you have to do for yourself. No amount of money can buy an attitude. No amount of influence can peddle one. You are the only one that can do it.

To conquer procrastination, you must develop the attitude that says:

- ✓ I will make no more excuses.
- ✓ I'll just do it.
- ✓ If I don't do as well as I had hoped, I will do better next time.
- ✓ I decide for myself that I am responsible for my failures.
- ✓ In the same way, I and only I can be responsible for my successes.
- ✓ When it comes to beating procrastination, I will succeed without excuse.

Of all the things that will help you break that cycle of procrastination, possibly the most significant is developing a little passion. When you find it difficult to get motivated and reach your potential, it is often because a sense of life apathy has set in our thoughts. Dr. Charles Garfield, in his book *Peak Performers*, studied people who have achieved significant, even phenomenal success. He makes a rather stunning statement when he writes, "Peak performers are people who really understand that the best use of a life is committed action to a mission that they care deeply about."

That really is a staggering assertion. We might expect that these peak performers have certain similarities in education, IQ, temperament, personality, family background, or social status. We might anticipate that their success is related to experience, talent, looks, good fortune, or inside connections. But the driving force behind significant success is the belief that what you are doing has real significance.

That is passion. Do you believe, or have a conviction that what you are doing matters? James Barrie says, "Nothing is work unless you would rather be doing something else." It is that kind of spirit that has led to some of the most phenomenal success stories we have known.

Man on the moon

One of the more famous stories and spectacular accomplishments is the dramatic assemblage of the NASA team to put the first man on the moon. When President John F. Kennedy announced in the early 1960s that Americans would be the first to put a man on the moon, it was quite literally an impossible task. There was no technology available that would allow us to do that. It was simply a bold and dramatic statement of vision.

What followed was a testimony to the power of the human spirit to rally around a cause, to find the motivation and accomplish what seemed to be an impossible task. The passion for reaching the visionary goal proclaimed by Kennedy made procrastination impossible. Those on the NASA team were driven to change the world - "what if" and "but" had no place in their vocabulary.

Yet you might say, "Great for them! But I don't have a glamorous job with world-changing implications!" This is all the more reason for you to find passion in your life.

The big picture

When you know where you are going and you continually focus on the big picture, there's no reason to put things off. It is the kind of spirit that produces peak performance. This kind of spirit leads to personal financial freedom as well.

Ask yourself this question - how passionate is my attitude for life? It may have more impact than you imagine.

We ran across an interview of a well-known actress describing how her friends used to try to talk her out of being an actress. She lit up as she said, "If someone doesn't have a passion – whether it's playing guitar or manipulating the stock market – you can't explain it to him or her, because it's got nothing to do with practicality."

To overcome procrastination, or even more significantly, to move toward realizing your personal potential, find your niche. This allows you to know that you are contributing something in this big, impersonal world.

Maybe it's an attitude that says, "I'm not just a teacher, I'm the molder of young minds and spirits that will one day be doctors, lawyers, pastors, CEO's, and presidents."

Maybe it's an attitude that says, "I'm not just a mother raising kids. I'm the primary influence on my kids concerning God, values, love, and relationships in life." For me, it's helping people grow in character and confidence as they find financial freedom, and helping people discover the reality and the relevance of a vital relationship with God.

It's not really what you do that matters, but the spirit and the attitude with which you do it. If you cannot find that passion in what you're doing now, do something else. Whatever you do, make sure to find your passion.

You may find it to help improve your life in a variety of areas, not the least of which is procrastination. There is a dangerous way of thinking in today's world. It is dangerous because it is self-deceptive. Because of its deception, many do not even recognize it as procrastination, and this may lend to its being the worst kind of procrastinating. We call it the "when/then" principal: "When I get ____, then I will ____."

Fill in the blanks with anything you like.

> ➢ When I get a million dollars, then I will be happy.

> ➢ When I have more time, then I will start Building my Business.

> ➢ When it starts affecting my job, then I'll quit drinking.

> ➢ When my wife begins treating me well, then I will treat her well.

When I _____, then I'll _____. On and on we could go.

I'm not describing the idea of rewarding ourselves for achieving. That method of motivation says, "When I accomplish my goal of making 10 phone calls this week, then I will reward myself with dinner out Friday evening." That can be helpful in causing you to stay diligent toward reaching your goals. If dangling these types of rewards can prompt you to accomplish more, then by all means do it.

But I am describing a much more sinister self-deception, which is the "when/then" principle. The "when/then" principle is not about rewards; it is about character.

For instance, I often hear people say, "When I get caught up at work, I'll begin building my business." Others say, "When I get my finances in order, I'll attend the next major event." Still others say, "When I get more time in my schedule, I'll begin listening to tapes and reading books."

If you don't do those things now, it's unlikely that you will do them when circumstances change.

Why?

Because we're talking about character.

We're talking about values.

Procrastination can be a most difficult pattern to break, especially when it deals with a fundamental need for character change. Quit saying "when/then," and begin developing your "now/now" attitude. That is the "now/now" principal.

Don't make your happiness, your good will, your habits, your integrity, or anything else conditional. Make your happiness, your good will, your habits, your integrity, or anything else absolute.

Do it now because it is right. Do it now because it is you. Do it now because it is your character. That will beat procrastination at its roots.

If you really crave breaking the cycle of procrastination, it's not complicated. But it's also not easy. Make a conscious decision to do it. Begin today. Hold yourself accountable to someone who knows you well. Then stop making excuses and attack life with a passion.

Have someone to call everyday to receive a positive input and encouragement as you implement your business plan. Project forward, using a multiplier, to visualize just how successful you will be in the future as you duplicate each small success you have achieved with your new attitude and work ethic.

You will succeed in this business, and in life, once you truly believe you can. So make a quality decision to get started - and never, never quit.

9

Hitting The Wall

By Doug Wead

L ife is like flying an airplane - hours and hours of pure boredom, interrupted by seconds of pure terror. Just when life settles into a routine, when even success no longer provides a thrill, those moments of terror will come, and one will learn very quickly how emotionally fragile, how close to total despair and death we really are.

How should we handle defeat and setbacks?

- What do we do when a heart attack or reports of cancer hit us?
- What can we do when tragedy strikes someone we love or hits our own crucial relationships?
- What is the formula for dealing with bankruptcy or allegations of wrong- doing?
- How do you fight your way back form alcoholism, or drug addiction, or imprisonment?

Here are three practical rules for putting setbacks into perspective. Being ready so that a defeat will not represent the knockout blow.

No problem can break you unless you let it

Keep in mind that all problems, all pain, all hurt is a passing experience. Hinduism and Buddhism preach this concept effectively but all religions, including Islam, Judaism and Christianity address it. And Robert Ringer and other writers of the 1970s pressed the point as secularists and atheists. Almost all problems will pass, and they cannot usually destroy you unless you panic and pull the plug on your own life-support. You will survive if you hang on.

Look out into the nighttime sky and consider the starlight that is coming to you from thousands of years past. In your mind's eye, soar out into the universe, past eons of stars, past their own solar systems of planets, traveling at the speed of light, hurdling deeper into the night. What is your problem, your embarrassment, your pain in the context of the vast universe? It is small, it is insignificant and it can be endured.

As a person of deep faith, I enjoy a small personal ritual that I have developed over the years. When I fly to Geneva, I try to stay at the Noga Hilton or another hotel overlooking the lake, with the majestic Swiss Alps rising behind it. I will tip the porter, shut the hotel door and then walk out alone onto the balcony to face the mountains. Their colors change dramatically, depending on the sun and the time of day.

I look at these giant mountains that have seen so many people come and go, that saw the armies of Hannibal and watched Napoleon slip through a pass and catch the Austrian armies off balance. I will say, based on a small Bible verse in Ephesians, "Long before you ever existed, God chose me. And long after you are gone, I will be. Because I am eternal, my soul will live on forever."

In most cases, the problems that you and I are experiencing today cannot destroy us - unless we let them. We have the power to pull the plug on our lives, to give up, to kill our own dreams. But no other authority - not divorce, not bankruptcy, not any government - has that power. Jesus once said, "Do not fear he who can kill the body and do no more." And He immediately offered the illustration of God knowing when even a sparrow falls dead to the ground. "Don't worry," Jesus said, "you are worth many sparrows."

There is opportunity in every problem

Much of what Sigmund Freud concluded more than 100 years ago has been discredited and dismissed by modern psychologists, but some basics remain. Freud found that all art sprang from the self-defense mechanism of sublimation. The artist used his or her pain, rejection, and frustration to ignite a brief burst of energy, achieving something truly creative. A generation later, William James concluded that this was the secret to all success, whether in the fields of education, government, military, or business. One does not need to sustain a torrid pace forever; one only needs a brief burst of power or energy, a few months of sustained, creative work to achieve a success that will last a lifetime. The idea is to "use" or "sublimate" the pain. Napoleon Hill talks about this in his classic book, *Think and Grow Rich*.

In rural India, on the Asian subcontinent, one can see the woman sitting on their haunches making little patties or pancakes out of the mounds of manure. Within hours, those patties will cover the hillsides, drying in the breezes and the warm afternoon sunlight. In the evening, when they are dry, the women will light them and they will slowly burn, providing a crude form of fuel. They become the burners to cook their food, or they may be lit to heat rocks that will keep a family warm on a cold village street. This is basically the principle behind all energy. It is this principle that lights up the city of New York tonight - all the manure, skin, bones and death, mixed with a billion years' time, produce the fossil fuels that provide the energy to run a modern city. It is a principle of life and business. Light, life, and energy springs from death, failure, and pain.

In the 1970s, Captain Jeremiah Denton was a prisoner of war in Vietnam. His captors presented him to the international press as proof American prisoners were being treated fairly. As he appeared before the media, Captain Denton stood stiffly, somewhat nervously, his eyes blinking wildly but saying all the things the North Vietnamese wanted said.

Weeks later, an American analyst suddenly hit on what Denton was doing. The analyst retrieved the videotaped press conference and studied it again. Just as he suspected, Denton was signaling Morse code with his blinking eyes, spelling out the message, "I have been tortured." The videotape was quietly shown in embassies around the world to influence neutral countries and force the North Vietnamese to provide better treatment.

The greater the problem, the greater the recovery - if you can just survive

Friedrich Nietzsche created the famous line, "what does not kill me only makes me stronger." It is a principle of life and nature, and it works in the emotions of men as well as on their bodies.

Here's how: when you are in the middle of pain, it is hard to see any value or use for your suffering. But history and life provide endless examples. Bad can spring from good and good can spring from bad. When modern sewage systems were introduced in many of the world's largest cities, a new, modern disease broke out across the civilized world - polio.

This new disease took tens of thousands of lives and left many others crippled. The children of previous generations, who had played in the streets, with sewage running under their feet, had the advantage of immunity from exposure to so many poisons.

Ironically, the new cleanliness of modern cities allowed a more sophisticated disease to run rampant. Eventually, a vaccine was found, taken from the disease itself and polio was eradicated.

But the lesson remains - solve one problem and get another, tougher one. End one pain and have it break out somewhere else. One cannot stop this ongoing process of life. It's like swimming in the ocean. It's better to ride the waves and use the rhythms to your advantage.

In the Jewish account of the Exodus, Moses makes an interesting philosophical point, right in the middle of his long narrative of his contest with Pharaoh. The Egyptians were angry and had decided that the Israeli slaves had too much time on their hands to think about freedom.

So they doubled the workload, ordering the production of twice as many bricks with even fewer resources. Moses, the historian, states the simple truth without a pause in his narrative. "The more they afflicted them, the more they multiplied and grew," he wrote.

Keep in mind that adversity is the fuel for greatness. The mosquitoes that survive this year's insecticides will drink them out of champagne glasses next year, because they will have developed immunity. The harder you throw a basketball against the wall, the greater the rebound. Remember Sigmund Freud's great discovery - artists used their pain to create!

Keep these three principles in mind:

1. No problem can break you unless you let it.

2. In every problem, there is an opportunity.

3. The greater the problem, the greater the recovery will be - if you can just hang on and survive.

Take time now, before failure hits, to plan how you would bounce back and what you would do. "Oh no," say some, one cannot even think about failure, let alone allow the word to pass one's lips. Our thoughts and fears will only bring such failures to pass. It's negative to even consider a worst-case scenario. But the key here is to anticipate a failure *with* a strategy to come out of it, and to have such contingency plans ready before they are ever needed.

All relationships, all careers, all causes will experience setbacks. Anticipating them with contingencies ready is not negative thinking - it is solid preparation. A little thought and commitment now may help you avoid your crisis later.

Careful and detailed planning for an eventual nuclear exchange is what helped the superpowers avoid just that for decades during the Cold War. And now, democracies and open markets flourish where stifling regimes once ruled.

Talk about opportunities arising from suffering!

10

Make It Happen

By Brian & Marg Hays

M ake It Happen people are the ones who exemplify the Always Positive Attitude and get the job done. Most of us would like to become more like these Make It Happen people, but we don't always understand what it takes to be in this elite group.

Make It Happen people come in all sizes, shapes, ages, colors, educational levels, genders, social backgrounds and economic levels. We cannot distinguish these results-driven people by outward appearances. This is definitely an "inside" job. They have developed the success traits of vision, discipline, example, positive attitude, persistence, right actions, commitment, determination, and resiliency. These qualities are there on the inside before the results are obvious on the outside.

They manifest themselves in the three-step process of all achievement:

- ✓ The Dream
- ✓ The Plan
- ✓ The Action

By learning and applying these, you no longer have to watch it happen or wonder what happened. You can Make It Happen.

You "gotta" have a dream

To become a Make It Happen person, we really need to know what "It" is. So, what is "It"?

It is our Dream.

"It" can be as specific and short-term as:

- Achieving your all-time high in sales
- Organizing a charity drive
- Losing certain number of pounds by your class reunion
- Remodeling your home

Or "It" can be as long-term and life-changing as:

- ➤ Becoming debt-free
- ➤ Building a successful business
- ➤ Devoting your life to a mission or cause
- ➤ Being free and owning your own life

The more long-term and life-changing your "It" is, the deeper and more passionate your desire must be. Our personal core values and beliefs are from a Christian worldview. We know our dreams must be in accordance with our faith. So, for us, our biggest dreams require the deepest assurance of our faith. When we base our dreams on that, we know we have the right "It", and we are committed to Make It Happen. We pray like it all depends on God and work like it all depends on us. Whatever your dream is, we challenge you to make "It" worth achieving! A dream worth achieving should be a dream worth keeping.

A make it happen person has a dream

I have always believed that the definition of success is the progressive realization of a worthwhile dream. Until a person has a clear-cut vision of what he wants, he or she never seems to have the motivation and energy to accomplish much in life. A person's dreams give them the purpose and reason to get up every day and "get going". There is an old saying, "If the dream is big enough, the facts don't count." We all need a dream to become our best self. In the play *South Pacific*, the song "Happy Talk" says it so well: "You gotta have a dream.

If you don't have a dream, how you gonna make a dream come true?" This is certainly true. We like to remind people to dream big Dreams. Big Dreams can stir your soul. Shoot for the stars. You'll at least hit the top of the telephone pole. If you aim for the top of the telephone pole, you might shoot yourself in the foot!

Visualize, crystallize and hold a clear picture of your dream in your mind. This is paramount to success. Remind yourself of your dream every day. Put up pictures of your dream (new car, home, new baby, vacation) on your mirror and refrigerator. Test-drive that dream car. Tour the new home. Gather travel posters. The more you involve the senses - touch, smell, sight and hearing - the more real your dream becomes. The more real your dream is, the more motivated and focused you are on achieving your Dream.

A Make It Happen person can't have a casual commitment that "I'm going to try" to accomplish my dream or say "Gee, it would be nice if I could achieve this." There is a cute story of a chicken and a pig going out to eat. They notice a sign in the restaurant window for a charity breakfast featuring bacon and eggs.

The chicken said, *"Let's go help out. We can make a contribution. I can contribute the eggs and you can contribute the bacon."* The pig replied, *"For you that is a contribution; for me that is a total commitment."*

Make It Happen people make a total commitment to their Dream. They are determined to get the job done. It's a decision of "whatever it takes." There is no backing down. We believe if you throw your heart into your dream, your body will follow. One person committed to a great idea can change the world. Indeed, it is the only thing that can.

We have found the minute you become a person in pursuit of a dream, the masses start to tell you it won't work. They try to steal your dream with ridicule and laughter. Some of our greatest accomplishments came when we had the most people laughing at us. This laughter is the greatest compliment you can receive, as it means you had the courage to step away from the crowd of the "Watch It Happen" and "Wonder What Happened" people.

Remember, people laughed at Henry Ford and his dream of a horseless carriage. They laughed at Edison and his dream of a light bulb. They laughed at the Wright brothers and their dream that we could fly. Thank God for dreamers - they have blessed our lives!

Don't let anyone steal your dream! They can only steal your dream if you stop believing. Don't give "them" control over your future. Don't get hung up on what "they" think about you. "They" don't pay your bills or care about your future like you do.

You need to associate with other dreamers because they will provide encouragement. Many times they will even give you constructive ideas to overcome the obstacles and challenges you are encountering. They may even provide personal help. Success breeds success; birds of a feather flock together. Seek out encouraging people. Surround yourself with the precious few who believe in you. If you are fortunate, you may find a mentor or role model to coach you through to your dreams.

Stick with the balcony people - the people who lift your sights and cheer you on. Stay clear of the basement people. You will have to overcome these basement people, these naysayers and scoffers. Don't get caught in the downdraft of doubt. They will always be there to drag you down, and they will always "Wonder What Happened" when they see your success as a Make It Happen person.

We had neighbors who constantly complained of having no money. When we began our business, we asked them to join us, to make some money for themselves. They declined, saying they didn't think it would work, but would watch us and see how we did.

When we got our first check for over $1500, we rushed over to show them. Then they said it probably wouldn't last, but they would watch us to see how we did. They may still be watching, but we are still Making It Happen.

To plan is to believe

One of the major things that sets apart a Make It Happen person is the ability to see the Dream clearly - and then develop a plan of action to accomplish it. If you fail to plan, you plan to fail. This has been proven over and over. He who aims at nothing is sure to hit it!

The Dream is what we want to accomplish. The goals are the measuring devices to get us to our Dreams. Goals take us step-by-step toward our Dreams. Goals are the feet on the journey toward our Dreams. They are the rungs on our ladder to the stars. Make It Happen people develop the ability to picture the results they want and also picture the steps they need to take.

Goals need to be precise, clear and written down. A target date for their completion is essential. Although our goals should stretch us, they also need to be believable and achievable. Otherwise, we discourage ourselves by unrealistic expectations. "Whatever the mind of man can conceive and believe, he can achieve," as the saying goes. Conceiving the idea gets us excited...but believing it gets us into action.

-   What do you need to do to Make It Happen?

-   What needs to get done?

-   What are the tasks to get you from where you are to where you want to be?

You need an understanding of the Basics in order to achieve the Big Times. You will need to get personally good at the Basics. The more Basics you can do well (not perfectly, but well) the more you can lead by example. Then you qualify to teach others by your experience, or expertise.

The famous Green Bay Packers coach, Vince Lombardi, once tried to refocus his team. He picked up the pigskin and announced clearly, "Men, this is a football!" That is getting back to Basics - know what game you are playing.

Equip your team

One of the best ways to get good at the Basics is through an education system of cassette tapes, CDs, literature, books, videos, seminars and communication. Stay connected to the techniques that work. Share successful experiences. Keep up your motivation. Become an expert. All these happen through an education system.

When you are in planning stage, remember to think of special tools and events to equip yourself and others to make the job easier. This approach gives hope, confidence, and enthusiasm and gets people moving. Conventions, seminars, workshops, retreats - all these develop esprit d' corps, an intense focus and concentrated learning. They are also primary for recognition, achievements and next-step focus. Enthusiasm bolsters our belief and makes every goal more achievable. We like to say enthusiasm is like the measles – contagious. There is tremendous value in an education system as you make your plans.

Most of us need a visual aide to help us clearly see the Basics. A spreadsheet, a graph, a chart, and a wheel – some kind of visual where you can set down in writing the components you need to master. Usually, we have already started our quest for our Dream when we take the time to do this.

Here's how:

✓ Write down what you already have accomplished.

✓ Write down what you believe you need to improve.

✓ Write down what are your goals for each of the Basics.

After the goals are in place, we now must determine the necessary plan to achieve them. We need to determine what actions will move us toward our dreams. Our goals should be set in concrete, but our plans in sand. Our best-laid plans can go astray. Sometimes, Plan A, the one that we carefully developed, can run into a roadblock. Many times, we need Plans B and C to detour around these roadblocks. A road map (plan) doesn't usually show the road under construction or that a bridge is out of service.

We don't see the roadblocks until we start down the road. We need to tweak and adjust and navigate some detours day-by-day. The Make It Happen person thrives on problem solving while executing the plan. They look for a solution to each challenge. They learn to roll with the punches, while other people roll over and play dead at these challenges.

Your Dream must be big enough to overcome the obstacles

Your life will always have obstacles; how much better it is to have Dreams to focus on, rather than focusing on the obstacles!

Be creative in your plans. Think of 10 ways to accomplish the goal. Possibility Thinking, which we learned from Dr. Robert Schuller, says, "When faced with a mountain, I will not quit. I will find a way over, under, around, through or with God's help, stay and turn the mountain into a gold mine."

Think of 10 ways to accomplish your goal. Use your imagination, calculate, break it into bite-size pieces. Bring to mind the obstacles you may encounter, then try to think of ways to overcome them.

While there is normally not a perfect plan from the beginning, we can often save ourselves a lot of mistakes by involving others in the planning stage. Different people bring a variety of experiences to the table and helpful insights that we might never think of on our own. When others are involved in the planning, many end up joining us in a common goal and often go further than just suggesting ideas. Many of them end up providing important resources, contacts, and even personal effort.

Make It Happen people are inspiring

They have a great ability to build teams around them, share their plans, and let these people share in the benefits with them. This is the perfect opportunity to involve others. In reality, most of our dreams do involve other people. For example, one of our dreams was for Marg to be a stay-at-home mom. We chose to earn money by developing a home-based business. We were looking for more time with our children and flexible hours.

As it turned out, our children became part of our business. They worked right alongside us, and shared in our success. This taught us an important lesson. One of the most important elements in long-term Make It Happen is to Make It "Happy." Plan for lots of celebrations. Celebrate each little success - for yourself, and the team of people who are on the Dream Adventure with you.

Recognize efforts as well as achievements. Getting people into action means giving them small, specific, achievable activities that they can do. Attach rewards to each activity. What gets measured and rewarded gets done. Make your plan work by giving such rewards as recognition in front of peers, pins, trophies, cash incentives, special dinners and award trips.

Seeing results gives motivation to continue on. I like to compare these celebrations to the fireworks displays we love on the Fourth of July. There are small celebrations for basic activities such as making a sale. You need to reward lots of these activities for lots of people. They're like sparklers - lots of sparklers make a good display when they're held in lots of hands. Then there are the ground effects – a little more impact and brighter than the sparklers. These are for important goals achieved along the way.

For the grand finale, you need skyrockets to make the big impact. It's the big celebration for achieving the dream. Make these grand finale fireworks bright, exciting, noisy and worth the achievement. This is the OOOOOHHs and AAAHHHs effect we all remember in the flashes and colors exploding in the night sky.

This big celebration is what motivates others to set big dreams and picture their own big celebrations. Observing other people's celebrations, especially if you are involved at some level of achievement yourself, moves the Make It Happen person to Action.

ACTION = W.I.N.

Most people "talk the talk", but few "walk the walk". When it's all said and done, there is usually more said than done. What you do speaks so loudly; I can't hear what you say. These well-known sayings illustrate that ACTION is the only thing that counts in getting the job done. One of the biggest losses to mankind is a great idea never acted upon.

I can recall my high school basketball days when my girlfriend, now my wife, was a cheerleader and one of the cheers they did was spelling out "I want some A-C-T-I-O-N! What does it spell? ACTION! Give me some ACTION!"

This is a cheer that rings in the ears of all Make It Happen people. Following through on ACTION sets them apart from the masses that go through life wondering, "What happened?" Once you have crystallized your Dream, and established your Plan, it is time for ACTION.

When is the best time to get into ACTION? Now! "Do It Now" becomes the motto of the Make It Happen person. The ACTION needs to be seen as an adventure, as an exciting journey toward the land of your Dreams. Focus your mind on the rewards and not on the efforts. You don't have to be perfect to get started. Just get started, and you will get skills enough to succeed. If the eagle waited for the perfect conditions, it would never soar.

What holds us back from ACTION? Fear! The fear of failure. It's more than our egos can handle. The fact is that most things we achieve are made up of a string of failures along the way. Failing is OK. It is just a part of the experience needed to win. As our friend and author John Maxwell teaches, we need to "fail forward."

We need to learn from our mistakes, apply those lessons and do better next time. Forgive yourself, develop a sense of humor and press on. Forget about yesterday. Today is a new day.

So many people have the mindset they would like to live their Dreams, but have excuse after excuse on why they aren't doing something. They pray for opportunity and when it knocks, they won't even open the door.

Wonder What Happened people lack ambition

A lot of this is because people fall into a comfort zone of what they are used to doing; they won't reach out. They are afraid to stretch, learn new skills, and be uncomfortable for a while. They are afraid of other people's opinion and rejection, or worry about what others might think. The truth is most of these people whose opinion we worry so much about don't think of us at all!

The only real failure any of us have is not trying. We fail when we quit on our dreams. Every setback along the way is another bit of experience in finding new ways to achieve our goals. John Haggai says, "Leaders have the vision and courage to act, and thus, don't even think in terms of success or failure. They believe even failure becomes the stepping stone for the next achievement." Failure can actually build your confidence, as you fail forward.

I remember when my wife and I won our first Incentive Trip to Hawaii. A big part of making this possible was based on registering people into our business. Of course, a lot more people turned us down than joined us. I took a handful of sand from the beautiful beach adjacent to the pure blue shimmering ocean and let it pour out between my fingers. I told my wife each grain represented someone who told us "no" and I asked her if all this failure was worth it to be here together. Then I chased her into the warm ocean waters while thinking of many of those who said "no," shoveling snow back in Chicago.

We had made it happen even though we had more failures than success. We could live this Dream because we were willing to go through failure. We accepted failure as a part of the success process.

Many people look for the easiest short cuts to achieving success. They say, "Stove, give me some heat and I'll put in some wood." They want to start at the top and work up from there. They demand instant results, or else they move on to something new. In asking a friend once to join me in an idea in which we could make some money together, he refused saying, "I'll just wait till my ship comes in." I reminded him that before his ship could come in, he had better send one out. Success doesn't attack you as you lie on the couch.

Make It Happen people know there is no gain without pain!

They are willing to move into new areas where they are uncomfortable in order to reach their Dreams. They see the end result will be worth the effort of trying new things and getting out of their comfort zone. They can picture themselves achieving the Dream before they get there.

Make It Happen people are ACTION oriented. The motto becomes "If it is to be, it is up to me." Consistency is the hallmark of their accomplishments. They "keep on keeping on" when most people give up. *A trait of successful people is they continue to place one foot in front of the other.* Persistence is often the best way to "figure it out." Quitting is never an option. If they temporarily get down, they must get back up. *They must give and give and give before they get.* They understand that delayed gratification brings reward to mature leaders who do not quit.

Their performance is based on their commitment, not their feelings. A newspaper reporter once asked Bob Hope how, after thousands of performances, he could feel like going out and being funny each night. Bob Hope replied, "I don't get paid for feeling funny. I get paid for being funny." Make It Happen people are not motivated by the feeling or mood, but by results they want. Real winners perform after the mood leaves.

A fact of human nature is most of us have short attention spans. Setting out for a five-year goal may be a bit overwhelming and we either don't begin or we get discouraged quickly. It is difficult to imagine staying focused, disciplined and in action for that long a period.

Instead, you may have better results in breaking your five-year goal into three- to six-month "Campaigns." A Campaign is a concentrated, high-energy, all-out focus to accomplish a short-term goal. This short-term goal is, in most cases, an important step in the five-year journey.

When you succeed in your campaign it will energize you to go to the next level. Great ideas coupled with intense action produce unbelievable results.

In order to focus your attention and the attention of the people on your team, you may want to give a name to your campaign. The name gives a sense of what you want to achieve, such as Core Action Group, Walk For Life, MADD. (Mothers Against Drunk Driving), USA, Volunteer Corps and Peace Corps.

The program sets a theme. It needs to cast the vision, have clear-cut requirements, an easy-to-understand agenda, establish accountability, have a definite time period, and give desirable rewards.

A membership name gives a sense of belonging and achievement: names that inspire and require accomplishments. Think about these group names: Cheese Heads, Bleacher Bums, Dead Heads. They give a telling picture of their membership as well. Let's choose the group we want to emulate! Again, a clear-cut vision and a picture of your Dream, helps you to name your group and establishes the image for achievement.

A slogan can build up a group of people to get the job done.

- "it is to be, it's up to me"

- "When all else is equal, the difference is me"

- "If whatever it takes…"

These are all themes that have rallied us toward success. Think of your campaign as having a Mission Control Center. Be focused on your objectives and on the important people. Get just a little bit organized. The purpose of getting organized is to help you accomplish your dream. Lou Holtz, celebrated college football coach, teaches one of the most important mindsets for success. The WIN mindset focuses us on

> ➤ What's Important Now?

> ➤ Who's Important Now?

Set your priorities on WIN! Manage your time; keep track of all the people, meetings, deadlines, and goals. Don't let anyone slip through the cracks. Write down everything that you need to do to move ahead.

Make a "To Do" list every night before you go to bed, so you'll be focused for tomorrow.

Do the most important thing first, even if it is the most difficult. The best feeling in the world is to cross off those "To Dos" and know you're moving in the right direction. A sense of accomplishment today is the best encouragement for productive action tomorrow.

When you do What's Important Now, you will win.

People who join your campaign need communication - phone calls, notes, emails, faxes and meetings. These are your new members who deserve and require lots of time and direction. The amount of time you need to spend with people is in direct proportion to the amount of action and commitment they demonstrate. Too many times, we spend time trying to "waltz with the one who doesn't want to dance."

It is so easy to get caught up moving around and not moving ahead. Moving Around People set up elaborate filing systems – but have no prospects or orders to put into files. They learn a proven script for approaching a new person or a new client – but they never pick up the phone. They develop a list of 200 prospects but never talk to one person. They surf the web for incredible knowledge, but never make one sale.

I remember my roommate in college was having trouble learning how to study, so night after night his ACTION was to read books on how to study. As a result, he flunked out because he never got around to the action of studying! Just being on the right track is not good enough. You have to move; otherwise you'll get run over.

Our ACTION needs to be directed to doing those things that are most important in moving us toward our goal.

Moving Ahead people get into action, they:
- ✓ Get out of the house
- ✓ Pick up the phone
- ✓ Talk to someone new
- ✓ Make Dreams come true

Stir up some action and clean up the mess later! The Moving Ahead people – the ones in action - are the "<u>W</u>ho's <u>I</u>mportant <u>N</u>ow" people. Spend time, counsel and build up these WIN people. Get them involved at every level - planning, action, celebrations, and feedback.

Surround yourself with people who are:
- ✓ Committed to the cause
- ✓ Demonstrate this commitment by their actions
- ✓ Get results
- ✓ Bring out the best traits in you
- ✓ Fill in the gaps you lack

These team leaders are whom you have to work with, mentor, inspire, challenge, and help achieve their own goals. Their goals become the building blocks toward your own goals. There is an old saying, "If you help enough people get what they want, you will get what you want."

Every army needs many troops, but the generals usually determine the victories. You will find your generals by bringing in new people, tracking, giving clear direction, leading by example, mentoring, and developing by apprenticeship. Or, maybe the generals find you because you have a Dream, a vision, and a plan and are leading the action!

Dan Jansen, Olympic Gold Medallist Speed Skater, signed a "Persistence" plaque for us. He said, "When you have exhausted all the possibilities, remember this - you haven't!" When you have done all you can possibly do, leave room for the miraculous. The Bible quotes, "God is able to do immeasurably more than all we ask or imagine, according to His power that is at work within us."

We learned this lesson in a big way when we set our goal to develop twelve business groups. We had done everything we could possibly do. We fell short by one group. We missed our goal and we were extremely disappointed.

To our amazement, a big account came through on the very last day of the month to qualify group #12. The next week, we went to our mailbox and found a check from Hong Kong! A group we did not even know was in business with us had also qualified. That gave us thirteen qualifying groups, a miracle bonus, over and above the 12 we had set our Dreams on.

It's as if we are making all our deposits in the South Side Bank and the dividends come back from the North Side Bank. We believe God honors your faith put into ACTION.

A Make It Happen person never learns how to quit. This can be illustrating by the story of a battle between two opposing armies.

After a long day's fight, the Northern army had lost most of their men to injury or death. Finally the general called the bugler to sound retreat, as he knew they could no longer hold their mountain vantage point. The bugler immediately responded, but rather than sounding retreat, he played "Charge!"

The General turned to him and said, "Soldier, I said sound 'Retreat!'" Again he blasted out "Charge!" on his bugle. With that the enemy army fled in chaos into the countryside. When they had heard "Charge!" being blasted at them, they thought there were reinforcements coming, so they feared for their lives. The charging army won the battle.

The General was overwhelmed and he praised the bugler - his sounding "Charge!" caused them to defeat the enemy. Then he asked, "But why did you sound 'Charge!' when I gave you the order for 'Retreat?'" The bugler immediately replied, "Sir, I never learned 'Retreat.'"

Never give up on your Dreams. Plan for success and believe it's possible. Do whatever it takes. That's how you live life as a Make It Happen person being always positive while you build your business!

CHARGE!

11

The Power of a To Do List

By Burke Hedges

"You can't build a reputation on what you're going to do."
\- Henry Ford

Over the years, I've been asked what I would consider the single most effective strategy I use to succeed in business. Without question, it's my daily To Do List.

How can such a simple strategy be so effective for success? Because it reduces the complicated to the simple and it transforms ineffective activity into productivity in every area of our lives and businesses.

I once had the privilege to take a mentor study course called *The Search for Meaning to Life's Journey* with my dear friend and mentor, Naveen Khurana. He taught me the importance of action when he shared these profound words with me:

I CAN'T HEAR WHAT YOU SAY BECAUSE
WHAT YOU DO SPEAKS SO LOUDLY

In other words, our actions communicate volumes to other people about who we are. How do you want to be perceived by those you love and respect?

I'm going to share with you how I use a To Do List to achieve my goals and accelerate my productivity in my eight businesses and in my life. You will learn the same strategies many highly successful people use to assist them in staying at the very top of their field.

A journey of a thousand miles begins with a single step.

Whatever it is we wish to accomplish, we have to do in steps. Each step moves us farther along the journey we are traveling - until, finally, we reach our desired destination or objectives.

How can we get what we want, whether big or small, unless we make it a priority and put it in writing so our objectives become a clear and conscious choice?

Think about it. If you were going to the grocery store, would you make a list of the items you wanted? If you were in an unfamiliar city and you wanted directions to a well-known restaurant, would you write the directions down? Of course you would, wouldn't you?

A good friend of mind once said to me, "Burke, too many people overlook the obvious." If you currently don't have a To Do List strategy that you apply six days a week, then you may be overlooking the obvious first step to consistent success in areas of your business and life that are important to you.

Priority, target, deadline

One summer, my buddy Gary Markel decided to take a few of his friends on his private jet to the Bahamas for a few days of "R 'n R." On the trip were two dear friends of mine, Davey and Susan Johnson. I took the opportunity to ask Davey a question about his good friend and colleague Brian, who is the son of a billionaire.

My question to Davey was, "You know Brian and his family pretty well, don't you?" He said, "Yes, I do." I said, "Davey, if you were to ask Brian's father what he attributes his amazing success to, what would his reply be?" Davey, without hesitation, replied, "PRIORITY, TARGET, DEADLINE."

In other words, the billionaire's strategy was to make his objectives a priority; to know exactly what his goals were, so he would know when he had achieved them; and to have a completion date to reach those goals.

I found his answer to be simple, yet profound.

The same can be said about a daily To Do List. It is simple, yet very, <u>very</u> powerful. First, a To Do List allows you to schedule your PRIORITIES, instead of prioritizing your schedule. Because it is used daily, you will have a DEADLINE for completing the task. And by putting your actions in writing, you now have a TARGET of what you need to do so you will know when it is done.

Along the path of life and business, we're going to find tasks that, when neglected, will prevent us from achieving the success we desire. These are the everyday tasks that we need TO DO in order to move us closer to our goals. The last thing we want is to be distracted by frivolous activities that waste our time and move us away from our goals.

The way I like to deal with high, medium, and low-priority tasks is to acknowledge them and have a strategy to deal with them. I like to address each task one at a time – methodically, persistently, and consistently until I complete it.

What is a To Do List? It's a simple strategy of what you want to accomplish, based on your priorities, your goals, and your urgency to accomplish them.

You may ask, "Why are so many capable, smart people so casual about such a simple strategy if success in life and business is important to them?" I believe it's for the same reason too many people refuse to put their goals and dreams in writing.

I believe people avoid putting their goals and dreams in writing because they fear they won't be able to live up to them. Napoleon Hill said, "What the mind can conceive and believe, then you can achieve."

What does this mean in this context?

It means that when you really believe in a positive outcome, then it will happen for you. But what if the mind conceives and believes failure? What would the outcome be? It would be failure, wouldn't it?

If a person does not put his or her daily goals in writing, secretly he or she may be thinking, "If I write down a goal and don't accomplish it, that will mean I'm a failure. And if I'm a failure, that means I'm not going to be respected. And if I'm not respected, then that means I'm not going to be loved."

This kind of thinking sabotages our success. We are responsible not only for who we are, but, more importantly, for whom we become. We are responsible for our own quality of life. We are responsible for the contribution we make to our families and community. We are responsible for putting our daily goals in writing so the beauty of our dreams can become possible. A dream is like a string of precious pearls. Each pearl represents a goal. Each goal starts with a To Do List.

Is a balanced life important to you?

In my book, *You, Inc—Discover the CEO Within*, I discuss a significant principle for success called Balance Your Life. This principle is based on the 5 Fs of our lives. The 5 Fs are: Faith...Family...Friends...Fitness...Finances.

The first "F" is *Faith*. The very core of our existence is based on a strong and meaningful relationship with God. Without Him nothing is possible. But with Him, the unimaginable is achievable. I consider Faith to be the core of our purpose and fulfillment. A strong Faith is like the hub of a wheel and the other 4 Fs are the spokes. You must make time for God if you want Him to make time for you.

The second "F" is *Family*. Our family is a gift and we must not take it for granted. All the money and success in the world would be meaningless if we can't share it with someone we love. We must make time for our Family to have balance in our life.

The third "F" is *Fitness*. What good is it to have an abundance of prosperity if we are too physically or mentally ill to enjoy it? Make time to take care of yourself both physically and mentally.

The fourth "F" is *Friends*. My mother said to me when I was 13 years old, "Burkie, tell me who you hang out with, and I'll tell you who you are." Make time to associate with and nurture quality friends. The best definition I know of a true friend is - one who walks in when the rest of the world walks out.

The fifth and final "F" is *Finances*. God wants you to be rich. He wants you to be a good steward of your Finances. Unfortunately, I see too many people spending 80 % of their time "chasing" the "golden rabbit," and 20% of their time on the other 4 "Fs". Make time to find balance between your Finances and your Faith...your Family...your Fitness, and your Friends. Put your Finances into perspective and in order, and financial abundance will come your way.

Zig Zigler said, *"You are either a wondering generality or a meaningful specific."* When organizing and carrying out a To Do list, knowing your priorities is vital. The 5 "Fs" are the foundation for what gives me meaning and purpose in my daily action plan.

A "TO DO" strategy for your To Do List:

Allow me to show you how I organize and work my To Do List. I like to keep things simple, practical and productive. And everything in my To Do list revolves around any one or all of the five "Fs". Fun is also a must in everything I do. If you make it a point to have fun in everything you do and laugh at yourself every once in a while, then you're bound to enjoy the process. Otherwise, everything seems to be burden. As long as you're taking the time to do whatever it is you're doing, then take the time to do it right and enjoy the process. I like to categorize my To Do List in four parts:

- ✓ To Do: ➢ What I want to do
- ✓ Calls: ➢ People I want to call
- ✓ Appointments: ➢ People I have to meet or what I'm going to do
- ✓ Notes: ➢ What I want to know and remember

I prioritize each category by HIGH, MEDIUM and LOW levels of importance. The HIGH-PRIORITY items are crucial, time-sensitive tasks to be completed the day of the To Do List. The MEDIUM-PRIORITY items are those important tasks I want to accomplish within three days of the date of my To Do List. The LOW-PRIORITY items are those tasks I want to get done, but which are not crucial; I'd like to get them done within a week of writing them down. Obviously, a low-priority item can change to a medium- or high-priority item within days.

Here are a few examples of how I prioritize my tasks in my daily To Do List:

HIGH: Board of Directors meeting, lunch meeting with potential prospect, real estate closing, prayer time, 10 sales calls, schedule training session. Set up breakfast meeting with managers. Exercise.

MEDIUM: Specific sales call to specific prospect. Purchase gift for son. Prepare for meeting. Follow up on previous appointments. Schedule family time. Take Mercedes to get serviced. Send thank-you note to customer. Meet with legal staff. Get to the grocery store. Meet with staff about seminar promotion, etc.

LOW: Organize desk area. Get car detailed. Get to the dry cleaners. Lunch with a buddy. Practice golf. Go to the movies, take kids fishing, select next positive book to read. Meet with accountants. Get haircut, etc.

I measure my actions by the number of High, Medium, and Low priority items and my calls to make on my Daily To Do List. My goal is to complete six high-priority items on a daily basis, six days a week.

At first this may not sound like much, but if you have six HIGH-PRIORITY items you are completing every day, then by the end of the week you would have completed 36 productive items.

 ➢ By the end of a year - 1,872 items.

 ➢ By the end of 10 years -18,720 items.

Can you see how a daily To Do List can significantly accelerate your success rate in life and business over time?

After you've identified your High-Priority items for the day, list your Medium-Priority items, then your Low-Priority items. Later, I will show you how I organize and list them.

Inventory your priorities

It's helpful to create a laundry list of all your To Dos, Calls to Make, and Appointments for the week. Then organize them by Faith, Family, Friends, Fitness, and Finances. Take a blank 8.5x11-inch sheet of paper, turn it sideways, and divide it into five equal columns across. On the top of each column, write from left to right My Faith, My Family, My Friends, My Fitness and My Finances. Now write down in each column, without prioritizing, everything you want TO DO or you need to get DONE. Do it now!

This is an actual example of what my Inventory (partial) list looks like. **Burke's SAMPLE To Do Inventory of 5 F's** (Faith, Family, Friends, Fitness, Finance)

Faith

- Time in the Word every morning
- Church Service
- Prayer at meals
- Community Contribution
- Church Picnic and retreats
- Ministry for kids
- Funds For Youth Athletics (A Non Profit Company.)
- Golf Tourney
- Fund Raiser for under- privileged kids

Family (Spouse, 4 Children, Mom, Dad and others)

- Dinner time with kids
- Baseball
- Basketball
- Soccer
- Dance
- Family Day
- Boating
- Beach
- Movies
- Vacations
- School Activities
- School work
- Personal time with each child
- Date with spouse

Friends (Lots of Buddies)

- Golf Outings/ Tournaments
- Counseling
- Fellowship
- Fishing
- Lunch and Dinner
- Picnics and Gatherings

Fitness (Physical and Mental)

- Cardiovascular training
- Weight training
- Golf training
- Eat properly
- Drink 8 glasses of water
- Read positive books
- Read Bio's of successful people/leaders
- Listen to audio tapes of inspirational and influential teachers/ leaders
- Attend personal development seminars
- Dentist/Doctors office for check up

Finances (Businesses)

INTI Publishing, Inc.

- Board Meetings
- New Products Develop
- International Sales
- Mass Market Sales

BH Seminars

- INT'L seminars & workshops
- Key Note speeches

Equibore of America, Inc.

- Board Meetings
- New drill acquisition
- Legal and Acct. issues
- New bldg. Build out.

Interact Corporation

- Board Meetings
- Lazy Shoezan Develop.

Backbone Worldwide, Inc.

- Product develop & launch
- Client support strategies
- Marketing strategies – domestic and Int'l.

Burke Hedges Corporation. (Consulting services)

- Strategic Planning and Implementation for business owners

Two Restaurants

- Board Meetings

Real Estate Investing Co.

- 5 acre Development
- Acquisitions of new properties

Now that you have a list of all the things you want to do or need to get done, **I would like for you to yellow-pad it.**

Do you sometimes just like to do things the old-fashioned way? Me too! But I'm also a big user and proponent of all the high-tech gadgets available today.

For instance, I own two laptop computers, three desktop computers, a Palm Pilot PDA and fax machines. I'm on the Internet, I own two cellular phones, and the list goes on. And, naturally, I have the time management software to go with it, including the Franklin/Covey System and Microsoft Outlook.

But in spite of all these high-tech gadgets, I have found that the more things change, the more they stay the same. The best tool I have found to get things done is to use a yellow pad and pen. Why? Because I'm not inconvenienced by the impracticality of electronic gadgets when I'm on the move, when I'm thinking of things I want to do.

Think about it: you're driving down the road and you remember something you have to do or someone you should call. What are you going to do, boot up your laptop to type in what you want to do? I don't think so! You write it down and then at a later, more convenient time and place, you transfer the information to Microsoft Outlook or Palm Pilot. I suggest you go with what works for you; many people use a day planner, and if that's what you're comfortable with, by all means, use it. But a yellow pad is what works best for me when I'm on the move.

The first thing I like to do every Monday morning is to plan my week by updating my previous week's action items and adding to the current week's To Do List. I prioritize my list and, as Dr. Ron Jenson taught me, I list my priorities:

✓ What do I need to do?

✓ Who do I need to call?

✓ Who am I meeting with?

✓ Where do I need to be?

✓ What do I want to remember or note?

My calls, My notes and My appointments

I like to list and see all the calls I want to make for the day and week, starting with the most important ones first. The calls I make will often dictate whom I need to meet with and what I need to do.

The note section is for my ideas, phone numbers, directions and other important information I want to remember. I do a lot scribbling in this section.

My appointment section is divided into three parts: A.M. is between 6 a.m. and noon; P.M. is between noon and 6 p.m.; and Evening is between 6 p.m. and midnight. My strategy is to have one "Ultra" High Priority item in each six-hour time slot, six days a week. Naturally, this is not always possible. However, when I really want to pour it on in my businesses, I make it a point to have the A.M.s, P.M.s, and Evenings scheduled with high priority items. This is when I'm the most productive. Give this strategy a try some week - you will rock!

Climbing the tree

There's an old saying: There are two ways to get to the top of an oak tree. You can plant an acorn and sit on it for forty years, or you can climb to the top.

In other words, writing your list and sitting around doing nothing won't get your work done. It won't move you closer to your goals and dreams.

So here's my easy two-step advice:

1. Make your To Do List

2. Then DO it.

That's it. Simple, but profound. Make the list and do it. NO excuses.

Whether you're rich or poor, pretty or unattractive, CEO of Microsoft or a stay-at-home mother raising a family – we all have the same number of minutes in our day, the same number of hours in our week to get things done instead of putting them off. NO EXCUSES!

But people have excuses – excuses for not wanting to have more financial abundance. Excuses for not taking advantage of all the joy life has to offer. Excuses for ignoring their responsibility to become all that they are capable of being, doing, and having.

These excuses remind me of the guy who wanted to mow his grass. But his mower was broken. So he went next door to his neighbor's house and asked if he could use his lawn mower.

"Sorry," said the neighbor. "I can't lend you my lawn mower because my wife is cooking beef stroganoff."

Startled by his neighbor's response, the man asked, "What does your wife cooking beef stroganoff have to do with your lending me your lawn mower?"

The neighbor looked him square in the eye and replied, *"If I don't want to lend you my lawn mower, any excuse will do!"*

If you're going to make excuses, then make the excuse to make the deposits of your To Dos today so you may enjoy the rewards tomorrow—one-thousand-fold!

Bill Gates, without a doubt one of the most successful businessmen ever, tells us not to handle the same issue twice - in other words, get it done!

You must be decisive. You must decide which items are your priorities and then do them, not just put them off until later - because tomorrow may never come. Bill Gates adds that a good manager is "hands-on" - so put your hands on your list and DO it.

Cross it off and bring on the next one

One of the best ways to tackle the list is to take joy in the process of crossing it off. Each time you complete an item on your To Do List, cross it out. The more cross offs I have, the closer I'm moving toward my goals.

Sure, it's simple - but it's very rewarding, too. You will find that the pleasure of crossing items off motivates you to do even more.

But what happens when you find yourself putting off important tasks? What happens when you find yourself wasting valuable time squandering your day, rather than doing what you know you should be doing? My advice is, don't get down on yourself. Please forgive yourself because tomorrow is another day. Remember, every day is an opportunity to start something great. What a difference a day can make.

The Greek philosopher Sophocles once said, "Heaven never helps the person who will not act." It just goes to show you that some things never change, and that the key to success today is the same as it was more than two thousand years ago. Actions speak louder than words.

Are you getting things done or putting them off?

The natural assassin of opportunity is…

"PROCRASTINATION"

I call procrastination "the slow death" because it starves action to death, rather than dealing with it head on with one fatal blow.

I think one reason so many people are procrastinators, is that they think they have to accomplish a monumental task all at one sitting. Nothing could be further from the truth. The beauty of taking action is that small actions over time lead to huge results.

That's right: small actions over time lead to huge results.

The key here is consistency.

✓ Take inventory of the 5 Fs of your To Do List.

✓ Write out your To Do List.

Approach it consistently.

Cross out those items every day, one after the other. You will begin to experience the joy of getting significant results over time.

I want to emphasize the importance of persistence. It's probably one of the most underused and underrated words in the entire dictionary. The best definition of persistence I've heard comes from Newt Gingrich, who says, "Persistence is the hard work you do after you get tired of doing the hard work you already did."

In other words, persistence may not be glamorous, but it sure gets the job done! I think too many Americans today overvalue talent and undervalue persistence.

Tom Peters, in his best-selling book *In Search of Excellence*, analyzed hundreds of companies in order to discover the key principles that drive America's best-run enterprises. After years of research, Peters came up with eight attributes that great companies have in common. Of those eight, the number-one attribute for excellence is, in Peters' own words, "a bias for action."

The best companies don't just sit around and talk about doing something – THEY DO IT!

What about you? Do you have a "bias for action?"

Be like Nike - Just DO It.

Because if *you* don't do it, who will?

Get a big dream and change your life!

How can a dream backed up by a To Do List change your life? Just look at Markita Andrews, a Girl Scout who dreamed a big dream, wrote it down, and made it come true! If Markita can do it, you can, too. Here's her story.

Markita and her mother had always dreamed about traveling around the world. They'd often talk about their dream, and Markita's mother, who worked as a waitress, would often say to her, "I'll work hard and put you through college. Then you can make enough money to take us around the world. Fair enough?"

When Markita was thirteen years old, she read in her Girl Scout magazine that the girl who sold the most cookies would win a trip around the world for two, all expenses paid.

Suddenly, Markita's dream began to take shape into a vision. She could visualize herself selling boxes and boxes of cookies. She could visualize herself receiving first prize. Most of all, she could visualize herself and her mom traveling throughout Europe...Asia...the entire world!

Even though she was only thirteen years old, Markita instinctively knew that thinking and visualizing her dream wasn't enough. She knew she needed to map out a specific plan.

So with the help of her mother and her aunt, Markita began to develop a plan. They wrote a list of things Markita had to remember to do each time she went out to sell her cookies.

> *And each day after school, Markita changed from her school clothes into her Girl Scout uniform and started knocking on doors. At each door, she followed the items on her list. And, more often than not, she would make the sale.*
>
> *In one year's time, Markita sold 3,526 boxes of Girl Scout cookies and won her trip around the world. Over the next few years she went on to sell more than 42,000 boxes of cookies, starred in a Disney movie about her quest - and co-authored a best-selling book, How To Sell More Cookies, Condos, Cadillacs, Computers...and Everything Else!*

Is it fair to say that Markita Andrews dramatically increased the odds that she would accomplish her goals by setting them down on paper? I have to believe the answer is a resounding YES!

No regrets

What will happen if you refuse to do the little things today that make a huge difference tomorrow? The results may not be noticeable today or tomorrow, but over the long run I guarantee they'll have a profound impact on your life and your business.

Don't let regrets take the place of your dreams. It hurts to look back on your life and wish you'd had the courage to do the items on your To Do List – and know you could have done it, but you didn't.

As you progress, you'll find many distractions in your path. But there are equally as many victories, if you are ready for them. Remember, you're the one who controls your thoughts: You can think as victor or victim - the choice is yours.

I came across an anonymous poem that sums up the essence of my message to you. It's called, "What Have I Done Today?"

> I shall do so much in the years to come,
> But what have I done today?
> I shall give my gold in a princely sum,
> But what did I give today?
> I shall build a mansion in the sky,
> But what have I built today?
> It's sweet in idle dreams to bask,
> But if not I, who shall do the task?
> Yes, this is the question each soul must ask:
> What have I done today?

-   What have YOU done today?

-   What will YOU do today?

-   Who will YOU become tomorrow?

Remember what Henry Ford said: "You can't build a reputation on what you're GOING to do."

Now, just DO IT!

12

Never Know Fail

By Tim Templeton

*"Our greatest glory is not in never falling,
but in rising every time we fall."*
- Confucius

Most who have succeeded have had a champion. This person is an advocate, someone who offers encouragement through the good times and bad, thick and thin, highs and lows.

For me, that person was my father.

Bob Templeton was born in Fort Erie, Canada, a ferryboat ride across the Niagara River from Buffalo, New York. In 1927, when the International Peace Bridge was officially completed and opened, five-year-old Bobby Templeton and his Canadian classmates walked halfway across the bridge to meet and greet their American counterparts from Buffalo. My dad cut the ribbon that day, and it became the pattern for his life – cutting through whatever else lay before him.

He lived life to the fullest. But he also prepared me for his death by sharing, "Tim, when my time comes, don't grieve for me. I've had a good run. I've always lived life the way I wanted to." He influenced many and many influenced him. But there was one man who influenced my father the most. Tommy Mullins influence of my father began when he was just a boy during those pre-depression years.

Tommy Mullins

The story of Tommy Mullins and his simple message made such an impact on my father that it became part of his personality. I heard the story so much when I was growing up that it became part of my personality, too. Tommy's message was like the scene in the movie, *City Slickers*. It was the secret to life, the elusive "one thing," according to Jack Palance's character.

We're all looking for that "one thing." The search inspired me to develop this compilation of wisdom from great leaders and authors, with the words Always Positive as the operative phrase in the title. Every great leader who has shared a story in this book has also learned Tommy's secret - Never Know Fail.

Their advice comes down to this - keep an Always Positive attitude in your life and business, and Never Know Fail!

Back to Tommy, who was not a wealthy man by monetary standards. He was not a powerful man by worldly standards. In the little town of Fort Erie, he was not even an influential man by community standards.

Tommy was simply the bread man.

He sold bread on the streets of Fort Erie. He lived in a studio apartment. It wasn't much of a lifestyle. But Tommy had something that each of us desires and needs – an Always Positive attitude. Though some saw failure in Tommy's life, he used it as a learning experience. Along the way, he learned how to do something right by knowing what he did wrong.

He came up with the phrase, "I never knew fail."

Tommy grew up in Hartleypool, England, a mining town north of London. He stood no taller than five-foot-five, and had a ruddy complexion of a hard life. Every day, he wore the same clothes - a heavy black overcoat and knee-high black boots.

He walked the streets of Fort Erie, selling fresh bread for a nickel from his old wooden pushcart. Each day, he maneuvered his cart by my grandmother's house, while singing out with a thick British accent:

"Fresh bread. Fresh bread hot from the oven".

Early in the morning, he would make his delivery to my grandmother, a woman who never met a stranger. Right there, on my grandmother's porch, Tommy would share his Always Positive attitude with my grandmother and my father.

"How are you today, Tommy?" my grandmother would ask.

"Mrs. Templeton, my life and business is tremendous," Tommy would always reply, with a twinkle in his eye and a smile on his face

"I Never Knew Fail."

Everyone always looked forward to seeing Tommy and experiencing his uplifting attitude. Everyone – and I mean everyone - bought their bread from him every day.

Never know fail in your business – steps to be always positive

It has been my privilege to be a speaker and a coach for business people. Through my experience, I have identified three different "business endings," or attitudes, that overtake many individuals in the industry. My background and expertise in working with leaders and giving insights on how to create new relationships that lead to business opportunities has repeatedly demonstrated one crucial element. It is the one difficulty common to any business or industry – finding people to share in your opportunity.

To succeed, you must create business opportunities every day. I do this by helping people interact with others. I use the Golden Rule - understanding what it means to "put the relationship first." By doing so, I have watched thousands of people become more pro-active and confident, offering opportunities to everyone they encounter – even people they've just met.

People handle business opportunities according to their personalities. I put them in three general categories – Overwhelmers, Underwhelmers/Secret Agents and Running on Empty. After describing the characteristics of these groups, I will offer solutions that many have used to take on an attitude of being Always Positive, and, like Tommy - Never Know Fail.

Overwhelmers

These folks get so enthused and excited over their opportunity that they cannot understand why everyone they know and meet should not get involved – immediately. While I applaud and encourage this "take the hill" approach, Overwhelmers have several negatives.

They ask few (if any) questions, listen very little and absolutely steam-roll everyone. Consequently, members of this group unknowingly alienate most people. Because their Overwhelming personality doesn't create many new opportunities, Overwhelmers become disenchanted.

Soon, a vicious circle develops – disenchantment and increasing negativity cause Overwhelmers to create even fewer business opportunities. That leads to more disenchantment and negativity, and the downward cycle continues.

Underwhelmers/Secret agents

Because of the downward cycle, Overwhelmers often graduate and become Underwhelmers/Secret Agents. This group is going to get started next week...after it gets a few things in order...when there's a full moon.

You get the idea. In Mexico, there's a saying for this – *manana*. It means "tomorrow," and we all know that in this context, tomorrow never comes. When I speak to members of this group, they're usually bright and articulate. By all indications, they should do well in business – *manana*.

But tomorrow never comes, and they never seem to get around to building a business.

Running on empty

Members of this group are like marathoners that have hit the wall after 19 miles. There's still seven miles to go, but not for members of the Running on Empty crowd. They're out of gas. Many in this group have been successful by most standards in the business, but now find they have lost their "mojo."

People who "manipulate" others shouldn't feel good about their approach to the business. They definitely are putting the money before the relationship with people. Their priorities are simply out of order.

The answer is The Golden Rule –
Put the relationship first!

Perhaps you recognize some of these characteristics in yourself or someone else. Maybe someone in your business is suffering from this debilitating mindset. The solution is simple - put the relationship first. Simply reverse the order on how you mentally prepare and approach this business. Start putting the relationship with others before your opportunity.

Here's another way to look at it – take the dollar sign off your forehead. You won't be projecting that image to everyone you meet. Your entire approach will change. You'll start seeing people as individuals – not as leads.

Use this simple technique, and people will suddenly be drawn to you. You will not experience as much rejection, because you change your focus to other people. It is not about you. It's about the people you meet.

If you incorporate this simple but effective philosophy, and practice it in your business, it will take on a whole new meaning and direction. Every leader who has shared in this book has put the interests of others first, and monetary success has followed.

Think about what attracts you to leaders in the business. You recognize the interest they take in other people, either by personally witnessing it or hearing about it. You are actually amazed and uplifted that they are concerned for you personally, when you have the chance to meet them.

For those who have met the leaders, or worked with them, their approach has made an impact. You have incorporated some of their techniques in presenting the business to others, explaining the care and concern of leadership and how much you enjoy the people who work with you. It's the Golden Rule - do unto others, as you would have them do unto you.

It works. It makes this business fun, and will give you an Always Positive attitude and self-image. You'll take pride in your new approach, and it will create a Never Know Fail mindset.

The Golden Rule - When they say no –
How to maintain your dignity

Tommy Mullins didn't sell bread to everyone in the neighborhood. You won't be successful in convincing everyone to take advantage of your opportunity. None of us likes rejection. But this business is like any other business. We won't do business with everyone we meet. It's just that simple.

Invoking the Golden Rule into your approach to the business starts by understanding this reality - before you share your enthusiasm for the business with another person. If you believe the *relationship* should be first, and treat people as you want to be treated, consider the dynamics of Funnel Methodology.

Funnel methodology —understanding the ratios

Use the image of a funnel to characterize your relationships with people. Draw a picture of a funnel and write the number 100 at the top of the funnel. Write the word RELATIONSHIPS next to it. This represents a minimum of 100 personal relationships in your life. These are people you could meet on the street, and they would know your name.

You could call each one of these people with the following offer – over coffee, you'd like to "run a few things by them" (explain your business). If they like what they hear, you'll "take it a bit further (tell them a little more about the opportunity). If they're not interested, you'll leave it at that.

According to industry averages, about one-third will be interested - about 33 people out of the 100 you know. Just under the top of the funnel, about a third of the way from the top, draw a horizontal line. Write the number 33 in the space and add the word APPOINTMENTS next to it. This represents the number of people who will give you time to explain what you do.

Of the 33 who hear about the opportunity, about one-third will get involved with your business. That means about 10 people will ultimately say yes. Now, here's the fine print. These numbers will go up or down depending on your personal abilities. They will definitely go up if you are stressing the opportunity over the products. Underneath your horizontal line across the funnel and the number 33, draw another line. Write the number 10, and add the word INVOLVED just outside the funnel. On average, starting with 100 relationships, 33 will take the time to listen to your opportunity and 10 will get involved as a business builder. Those are the ones that will go to meetings and conferences, want to develop themselves personally and build a business.

9 out of 10 eventually may say no

If you buy into the above ratios (again, it depends on your personal abilities and if you are stressing the opportunity over products, your ratios will be much higher than if you are offering products), nine out of ten people you know and meet will say no. That equals a 90% rejection rate.

It's quite a hurdle to overcome, and will debilitate even the most optimistic personality. In fact, it automatically thrusts you into the mindset of the Underwhelming Secret Agent - **unless you put the relationship first, by invoking the Golden**

Rule.   If you have incorporated this simple but universally profound truth into your attitude and business, you will join the ranks of other successful leaders. You will know their secret – how to keep their relationships, friends, dignity and build a successful business at the same time!

Golden Rule/Golden Words

When one of your friends expresses a less-than-Always-Positive Attitude about your business, you can sincerely reply, "that's OK. Not everyone I know is actually suited to get involved in this business. I believe you should experience the products. But you make that decision. The relationship I have with you is more important than my products or business."

When you have the right perspective, the right attitude, and the right responses, you will be encouraged to take on and project Tommy's Always Positive, Never Know Fail attitude.

Filling the top of the funnel

As I mentioned earlier in this chapter, my expertise is helping people in this business make sure they always have new names for the top of the funnel. New names enables one to make new relationships, set appointments easily, build an organization with less stress and receive multiple referrals regularly.

So, how do you replenish the top of the funnel? It's simple - new relationships. Always be thinking, "if I don't know whom I'm going to talk to on Monday morning, I'm temporarily out of business until I do." If you grasp this simple process, the leadership that surrounds you will help you get those you know involved in your business – and move to the next level.

It's not about you;
It's about putting the spotlight on those you meet

Here's a simple process that will help you have more confidence when you meet someone. I guarantee that it works. The next time you meet someone, don't overwhelm them with your opportunity. Treat them as you would treat a new friend.

Remember, it's all about them. It's not about you.

I have worked with Mark Michalek, the number-one auto salesman in the world. He follows this motto - make a friend, sell a car. Let's make sure we understand the order:

- Make a friend
- Sell a car

The friendship comes first.

Mark is a regular guy with a blue-collar background out of Pittsburgh, Pennsylvania. His philosophy has propelled him to be the number one salesman in the world because it is based on the Golden Rule. It works for him, and it will work for you.

Here's the way to meet someone. Introduce yourself, and focus immediately on your new friend. Start by asking the four Magic Questions:

- What is it you do?
- What do you like most about that?
- What do your friends or associates like most about you?
- If you could start over, knowing what you know now, what would you be doing for a living?

Bonus Statement:

- Tell me more...

Then, sit back and enjoy the results.

Knowledge is power

Whether you share your business concept at that moment or wait for another time, your next move is always the same - go home and send a thank-you note explaining how much you enjoyed meeting and learning about your new friend. Immediately put this person's contact information in your database, Rolodex or notebook.

When you decide to follow up, asking if you could talk to them about your business, do you think you will have a more open-minded person? Absolutely.

You now have a blueprint of who that person is, what he or she does, what he or she believes what other people think, and his or her goals in life. With the knowledge you have gained, you are in a position to engage that person – not as a potential sale, but as someone with whom you have a relationship. Your newfound knowledge will give you a sense of empowerment and confidence.

Sherry's story

Sherry is an experienced professional in the business. After reading my book, *The Referral of a Lifetime*, Sherry called me and said, "You know all about meeting new people and building relationships. I want my whole team to learn about it."

Over several conference calls, I coached Sherry and her group. I covered the principles of putting the relationship first. I also coached implementation of the four Magic Questions.

Sherry tried out the questions on a flight to Hawaii. She was traveling to a conference, and the plane was half filled with people in the same business. At the beginning of the four-hour flight, she observed her counterparts overwhelming the unsuspecting tourists sitting next to them. With a chuckle, she told me the conversations between her counterparts and those seated next to them abruptly stopped about an hour into the flight. There would be no interaction between them for the remainder of the trip.

She was laughing, she said, because she was seeing herself in those situations. That was the way she once approached new contacts. She went on to explain how she simply asked the four Magic Questions to the fellow next to her, enjoyed the conversation and exchanged cards.

"I'd like to learn more about what you do," the man told Sherry. "I enjoyed meeting you. You're an interesting person with a very interesting lifestyle!"

Sherry laughed again. "Funny he should say that," she said. "We spent most of our time talking about him."

The Golden Rule makes you more interesting

When you put the relationship first and invoke the Golden Rule in your business, the result is nothing short of miraculous. People you meet will enjoy talking about themselves much more than listening to you.

They will enjoy the experience and be open to exchanging a business card or address. Because you are genuinely more interested in them, you will find they become more interested in you.

I have coached many people, and I know it works. People tell me the same story - this simple process has helped so many expand their business. Incidentally, Sherry later called the fellow sitting next to her on the plane. He took her call enthusiastically, and did get involved with her in business.

Follow the leaders...Who never knew fail

This book is a compilation of the insights of leaders who have found huge success in business and have a deep desire to see you succeed as well. They have experienced great hurdles, like the ones you are or may face one day.

Their stories are your stories. By incorporating their successful strategies, you can be encouraging to everyone in your personal and business profession. Here are several summary highlights:

Jim Dornan, *A Healthy Self Image-Chapter 2*

As you develop your healthy self-image, you'll discover the balance between:

- a sense of peace
- a sense of purpose
- a sense of humor

Here's how to build a healthy self-image:

- Continuing to pursue a dream when others are quitting all around you
- Continuing to get up
- Making small progress when you feel the destructive power of doubt
- Realizing any little success means progress
- Earning the respect of your peers in your industry or team
- Feeling satisfaction when you overcome a fear or solve a problem on your own
- Doing something well the first time you try it

A healthy self-image checklist:

- Identify your strengths (and weaknesses)...don't seek perfection
- Look beyond yourself to your Creator for a sense of value and purpose
- Don't be fooled by cultural pressure - what really matters?
- Discard the past, along with labels given by others
- Develop positive, constructive self-talk
- Protect your environment – Garbage In, Garbage Out
- Feed your potential with books, tapes and healthy associations
- Build on the small successes
- Find your areas of excellence as a foundation of confidence
- Be thankful if you find one person who makes you believe in yourself

Dr. Ron Jenson, *Living a Principle-Centered Life-Chapter 3*

Identify and build absolute values into your life and business. Your absolute values will give your strength, success, and significance. To do so you must:

- Verify your own values
- Articulate your universal principles
- Learn the right perspective on issues
- Unpack right values through action
- Evaluate your growth
- Share these truths with others
- Take action

Hal Gooch, *Identify Your What & Why-Chapter 4*

Four ways to become the best you can be:

- Take total responsibility for what you've been, what you are and what you will become
- Develop your own dreams
- Become obsessed with learning
- Seek our mentors and colleagues who will help bring out your best in the future

Four ways to stay flexible:

- Begin each day positively
- Keep goals constantly in front of you
- Keep reminding yourself why you want to succeed
- Be flexible, even in the area of criticism

Open-ended questions that will help you build your team by learning more about others:

- "Tell me more..."
- "What do you mean...?"
- "How will you...?"
- "If you were in my shoes, what would you...?
- "What do you think about...?"
- "How can I find out about...?"

Strive to be consistently better than anyone else in the following areas:

- Do more homework and preparation.
- Learn more.
- Do more exercise, and stay in the best physical shape possible
- Drive the cleanest car, and wear the cleanest, best-pressed clothes
- Be the most organized
- Be memorable

Beverly Sallee, *Visualize the Finish Line-Chapter 5*

- If you are poor...work
- If your health is threatened...work
- If disappointments come...work
- If you are rich, continue working
- If faith falters and reason fail...work
- If dreams are shattered and hope seems dead...work
- If sorrow overwhelms you and loved ones are untrue...work
- If you are burdened with seemingly unfair responsibilities...work
- If you are happy, keep right on working

Dr. Ron Jenson, *The Life Changing Impact of Mentors – Powerful Influences in Positive Thinking-Chapter 6*

When mentors get involved with people, they leave lasting legacies. Two simple questions to ask yourself:

- Are YOU seeing Lives Changed?
- Are YOU Believing in People?

Jack Daughery, *Self-Discipline Creates an Always Positive Attitude-Chapter 7*

Three steps to acquiring self-discipline:

- Transform your desires into a clear objective
- Consistently reinforce and repeat your decision each day with action and thought habits
- Immediately act when the opportunity to advance your objective presents itself daily

Ten principles to maintaining self-discipline:

- The Future is in Your Control
- The Responsibility for Success is Yours
- Make Daily Progress Toward Your Goal
- Focus on the Desired Goal for Success
- Your Mindset Determines Your Success
- Commit to the Race
- Stretch for Goals Higher than Yourself
- Accurate Thought is the Sign of a Self-Disciplined Mind
- Action Plan for Success
- Daily Habit Forces of a Self-Disciplined Mind

Jim Floor, *Get Out of the Vacuum and Build-Chapter 8*

Two steps to stop procrastinating:

- Stop making excuses and rationalizations
- Start immediately and don't stop

Three steps to staying healthy and on track:

- The lasting defeat of the problem of procrastination as a habit and hindrance
- Learning the life process of evaluating and eliminating the useless and damaging from your life
- Making discipline an essential and effective part of your character

Six bits of advice to pick you up when you think you failed:

- I will make no more excuses
- I'll just do it
- If I don't do as well as I had hoped, I will do better next time
- I decide for myself that I am responsible for my failures
- In the same way, I and only I can be responsible for my successes
- When it comes to beating procrastination, I will succeed without excuse

Doug Wead, *Hitting the Wall-Chapter 9*

Three principals that will get you through the tough times:

- No problem can break you unless you let it
- In every problem, there is an opportunity
- The greater the problem, the greater the recovery - if you can just hang on and survive

Brian and Marg Hays, *Make It Happen-Chapter 10*

The three kinds of people in the world:

- Those who Make It Happen
- Those who Watch It Happen
- Those who Wonder What Happened

Three steps to achievement:

- The Dream
- The Plan
- The Action

Three more characteristics of success:

- You Gotta Have a Dream
- To Plan is To Believe
- Action = W.I.N.

Burke Hedges, *The Power of a To Do List-Chapter 11*

The three secrets to taking control of your life:

-   Schedule your PRIORITIES, instead of prioritizing your schedule
-   TARGET in writing what you need to do, so you'll know when it's done
-   Do it daily to give yourself DEADLINES for completing the task

Remember to schedule time for The 5 Fs:

-   Faith
-   Family
-   Friends
-   Fitness
-   Finances

Becoming Always Positive while building your business is about being genuine. It's about continuing to grow as a person. It's about taking on Tommy's attitude of Never Know Fail. It is also about staying with it - through the good times and the bad times, thick and thin, the highs and the lows.

I wish I knew who wrote the following poem, because it has been my personal favorite for 25 years. I recite it regularly, and I hope you find it as inspiring as I do.

DON'T QUIT

WHEN THINGS GO WRONG
AS THEY SOMETIMES WILL
WHEN THE ROAD YOUR'RE TRUDGING
SEEMS ALL UPHILL
WHEN THE FUNDS ARE LOW
AND THE DEBTS ARE HIGH
AND YOU WANT TO SMILE
BUT YOU HAVE TO SIGH
If CARE IS PRESSING YOU
DOWN A BIT – REST IF YOU MUST

BUT DON'T YOU QUIT
LIFE IS QUEER WITH ITS TWISTS AND TURNS
AS EVERY ONE OF US SOMETIMES LEARNS
AND MANY A FAILURE TURNS ABOUT
WHEN YOU MIGHT HAVE WON
HAD YOU STUCK IT OUT
DON'T GIVE UP
THOUGH THE PACE SEEMS SLOW
YOU MAY SUCCEED WITH ANOTHER BLOW

SUCCESS IS FAILURE TURNED INSIDE OUT
IT'S THE SILVER TINT OF THE CLOUDS OF DOUBT
YOU NEVER CAN TELL HOW CLOSE YOU ARE
IT MAY BE NEAR WHEN IT SEEMS SO FAR

SO STICK TO THE FIGHT
WHEN YOU'RE HARDEST HIT
REST IF YOU MUST
BUT DON'T YOU QUIT!

Since I'm a coach, here's one final pep talk before I send you on your way.

- ✓ Follow in the Steps of the Successful Leaders Who Have Done It!

- ✓ Never Know Fail!

- ✓ ***Create and Maintain an Always Positive Attitude While You Build Your Business!***

Notes

Notes

Notes

Notes

Notes

Notes